Is There an Engineer Inside You?

A Comprehensive Guide to Career Decisions in Engineering

Celeste Baine

Bonamy Publishing, Calhoun, LA

Is There an Engineer Inside You?

A Comprehensive Guide to Career Decisions in Engineering

BY CELESTE BAINE

Published by:
Bonamy Publishing
P.O. Box 673
Calhoun, LA 71225 U.S.A.
(318) 644-0532

Printed in the United States of America

Publishers Cataloging-in-Publication
Baine, Celeste
        Is there an engineer inside you?: a comprehensive guide to career decisions in engineering / by Celeste Baine.
        p. cm
        LCCN: 98-96216
Includes bibliographical references and index.
        ISBN 0-9664763-0-1 (pbk.)
        1. engineering--vocational guidance
        2. career education--handbooks, manuals, etc.
        3. engineering--study and teaching "HIGHER"

How to Order:
Single copies may be ordered from Bonamy Publishing, P.O. Box 673, Calhoun, LA 71225; telephone (318) 644-0532. Quantity discounts are also available. On your letterhead, include information concerning the intended use of the books and the number of books you wish to purchase.

Acknowledgements

I want to extend my thanks and gratitude to the many professors, counselors, fellow students, and recent graduates for the information and contributions they have made to this work. I can not list every source consulted in the preparation of this manual, the list is too extensive.

Countless engineering societies have overloaded me with information and contributed enormously to this manuscript. Articles and information have been contributed by National Engineers Week, AIChE, ASME, ASHRAE, Student Publications of Kansas State University, IEEE, SME, ANS, ASHE, BMES, and many others.

I also want to thank my Mom, Dad, and Amy for their support, understanding, and encouragement.

Editing by Terry McConathy
Cover Design by Sharon Gaines

Table of Contents

Part II

Chapter 4

Chapter 5

Chapter 6

Chapter 7

Chapter 8

Chapter 9

Warning - Disclaimer

Although the author and publisher have attempted to research exhaustively all sources to ensure the accuracy and completeness of information on the subject matter, the author and publisher assume no responsibility for errors, inaccuracies, omissions, or any other inconsistencies herein.

The purpose of the manual is to complement and supplement other texts. You are urged to read all the available literature, learn as much as you can about the field of engineering, and adapt the information to your particular needs. There may be mistakes within this manual. Therefore, the text should be used only as a general guide and not as the ultimate source of engineering preparation and career information.

If you do not wish to be bound to the above statements, you may return this book to the publisher for a full refund.

Introduction

In 1993, I packed up everything that I owned and headed east to Louisiana to begin engineering school. I wanted to study biomedical engineering, and there weren't too many affordable programs around. I chose a small school so I could be taught by professors instead of graduate students. I hoped to visit these professors in their offices and make them remember me years from now.

I was very serious and worried about making A's in everything my first year. I thought my future employers needed a straight-A student. In my second calculus class, my ideal world began to slip away. All students have a class with professors they don't like or can't understand. This was my class. I finally met a professor I thought I couldn't learn from. He would lecture and tell jokes, but I couldn't laugh; his jokes weren't funny because I couldn't understand what he was trying to say. I would go home, struggle, and even cry when I tried to do his homework. Everyday, I forced myself to open my notes and try again. Most days, I felt like I was pounding my head against the wall. Maybe I was in the wrong major. Maybe engineering was for the elite. Maybe I didn't fit the model of what engineering students were supposed to be. At the time, I thought I knew why everyone complained about the difficulties associated with obtaining an engineering education. Today, I can tell you that I didn't really know then.

Thankfully, that class ended, and I went on in pursuit of my education. I was soon to find that the experience I gained from learning to deal with that difficult professor came in handy over the next two years. It is impossible to avoid all the professors you don't like. The strategy essential to getting through school is to become excellent at taking tests. If you can learn to temper your frustration and anger about a particular professor and streamline all your effort into passing tests, then no professor can stop you from achieving your goals. Try to see your professors from a different angle by visiting them in their office or emailing a class question. Sometimes a visit at their office can remind you that they are real people and not someone your imagination dreamed up to torture you for cutting class in the 10th grade. Fortunately, most professors genuinely want you to succeed.

A career in engineering is the perfect example of the American dream. When you tell your mom and dad you want to go to engineering school, they naturally beam with pride. Your friends and acquaintances suddenly put you in a different intellectual bracket than before. Everyone wishes you good luck as you leave for the first day of class.

There are numerous horror stories about the rigors of engineering training. However, that is not the focus of this book. The intention of this book is to focus on the new world of opportunities that will open up to you when school is over. This book is not written from the standpoint of an educator but from a student. Students, rather than educators, know what is interesting to other students and know what you need to know to get through this kind of program. It's an invaluable perspective you can't find in many books. This book doesn't focus on how a class is taught but on how to prepare for college and how to find the resources available to ensure you succeed. Engineering education is like a "right of passage." It opens the door to possibilities you never suspected existed. When you finish your degree, you are an engineer and you have the confidence and "know how" to become anything you want to be.

Richard Riley, the U.S. Secretary of Education for the U.S. Department of Education, said in a 1998 presentation for National Engineers week, "coming from the business world, engineers know what it takes to succeed. They know that the jobs that will be created from here on in will require workers who have a sound knowledge of math, science, and technology, and are problem-solving team players."

As technology increases, engineers need to become more versatile, adaptable, and social. Schools everywhere are changing their curriculums to include more teamwork and public speaking. Opening the want-ads demonstrates the need for excellent oral and written communication skills that can be seen in numerous job postings.

This book has developed out of my own desire to reject conventional stereotypes and models of engineers. In part, my rejection is forced because I'm a woman in a male-dominated field. I am an engineer and have many engineering friends who don't fit the ancient engineer, pocket-protector, thick glasses, and antisocial-nerd stereotype.

My other motivation for writing this book is to help you see that engineering can be fun. It's fun being on the cutting edge of technology, and it's exciting to try to make the world a better place to live.

It is true that there is an abundance of jobs out there for someone educated in engineering. It is true that if you keep up good grades, you can get almost any all-star job you want. But, do people need to take the traditional path and walk in the footsteps of the engineer before them? What about women and minorities in engineering? What about the person who has other skills that can add new dimensions to traditional engineering? What about the person who studies engineering only as a launching pad for a different career (such as environmental engineers who become attorneys and biomedical engineers who become physicians)?

This book is also my attempt to show you a handful of the most popular and dramatic career opportunities I've uncovered in my quest for alternatives. If you were to ask me today, I'd tell you that even though I don't do engineering on a daily basis, being an engineer is the best thing I've ever done in my life. Studying engineering, although painful at times, is also the best gift you can give to yourself. You will develop analytical and logical thinking skills that will help you in everything you do for the rest of your life. It will prepare you for your life like nothing else can.

Part I

What *is* Engineering?

Chapter 1

Surf's Up in Engineering

Engineering is one of the most progressive, challenging, and rewarding fields that can be studied today. Many people want to be an engineer. Almost everyone has the ability, but few possess the drive and perseverance. You might be asking yourself, "how do I get drive and perseverance?" Simply stated, you have to be willing to make the effort and not let anything stand in your way. You have to know what you are getting into and have a clear idea about what you want. This book will show you why you already have the ability to be an engineer, how to prepare for an engineering education, what to expect in college to give you an edge over your classmates, and what resources are available to aid your college preparation. The differences between each branch of engineering and what traditional and non-traditional opportunities exist only for engineers are also in this book. In addition, there is an extensive society reference in the appendix to enable you to find more information on the particular branch or specialty of engineering that interests you and an engineering camp directory to assist your early preparation.

Individuals with a bachelor's degree in engineering enjoy some of the highest paychecks of all baccalaureate graduates. The classified ads of every newspaper typically have several ads, if not whole columns, or pages of fabulous job opportunities for engineers. Engineering is the second largest profession in the nation with more than 1.8 million engineers in the workforce.

So, what is engineering? According to Jeff Lenard of the American Institute of Chemical Engineers (AIChE), the role of the engineer is perhaps one of the least understood in society. In any poll asking what engineers do, the responses invariably include "fix cars" and "drive trains." We see doctors, lawyers, and police on television, but what are engineers doing? According to the National Society of Professional Engineers (NSPE), "Engineering is the profession in which a knowledge of the mathematical and natural sciences, gained by study, experience, and practice, is applied with judgment to develop ways to utilize, economically, the materials and forces of nature for the benefit of mankind."

Scott Adams, the creator of the Dilbert comic strip, is trying to debunk the mystery of engineering. In an interview with the American Association for Engineering Education (ASEE), Adams said, "When I grew up, if you had mentioned engineering, I wouldn't have known what it was. But when you read Dilbert, whether you like it or you're afraid of it, you know what he's doing. You know he's in meetings: you know he's doing things with his computer: you know he's inventing things: you know he's working on things with marketing. You actually have a pretty good idea of what an engineer does."

Engineering is all around us and is most likely the best way to make the biggest contribution to society. Engineers work to improve the quality of life and to make life more efficient or comfortable. They strive for constant improvement by applying scientific principles to solve everyday or specialized problems in a practical way. Engineers may design products such as automobiles or design systems such as the roads, bridges, overpasses, and streets the automobiles travel on.

Not all engineering students are alike, and the engineering marketplace is no different. With more than 25 major branches of engineering and 100 specialties, there is something for everyone who pursues the engineering field. Your personal goals, skills, and personality will determine which branch or specialty of engineering is right for you.

People have always held engineers in high regard; after all, engineers make the world go around. The majority of all technological advances, such as televisions, computers, the internet, the space shuttle, and airplanes, can be attributed to the work of engineers. Prestige is also associated with the knowledge engineers have acquired through their commitment to finish college.

There is no standard of intelligence needed to complete a degree in engineering and there is no limit on the amount of time it takes to complete a degree. Some students take it slowly because of part-time jobs, family responsibilities, or simply the desire to excel in their classwork. An engineering student who is willing to work hard, to develop the necessary math and science skills to keep at it when things get tough, and to work smart can expect a nice paycheck as well as a challenging and stimulating career.

A degree in engineering can open many doors. People who want to improve society, reduce pollution, end world hunger, invent exciting cutting-edge technology, make life more convenient, or develop new theories to change the ways we think about the world need to consider a career in engineering seriously. Anyone who is up to the challenge and has a genuine interest in taking things apart, solving puzzles and problems, or understanding nature can succeed. The necessary skills to succeed in engineering school are attained by determination, perseverance, effort, and creative problem-solving (just like the skills necessary to be a competent engineer!). Excellent grades in math and science through high school (although nice to have) are not prerequisites to becoming a good engineer. Many high school students do not apply themselves but find out that, when they try to work on a stimulating problem, they enjoy the problem-solving process and the solution comes easily. If you feel you have the aptitude and make the commitment you can and will succeed in school.

Engineers apply math and science to solving problems. Suppose you are a B student in math and science but you excel at communicating. Traditionally, people would have steered you away from engineering. If you have the drive and motivation to get through those math and science courses, you could become one of the most valuable types of engineers because not many people can communicate the language of engineering to other non-technical persons. There is a tremendous need (just scan the job descriptions of most engineering positions) for the engineer with excellent verbal and written skills.

With a solid foundation provided by an engineering degree, a career in engineering can take you anywhere you want to go.

Who Chooses Engineering and Why

The engineering field is made up men and women from every different culture who want to help solve the world's problems. The only element that all engineers have in common is a desire to make the world a better place. Engineers can be married or single, they can have disabilities, and they often have different perspectives. Problem-solving orientation is the common factor. Engineering students can be right out of high school, just out of the military, returning to school after several years, or seeking a second degree.

Engineers also receive valuable preparation for a host of other careers such as finance, medicine, law, and management. These professions require analytical, integrative, and problem-solving abilities, all of which are part of an engineering education. Thus, engineering is an ideal undergraduate education for living and working in the technologically dependent society of the twenty-first century (The Green Report, Engineering Education for a Changing World).

A primary reason people choose to study engineering is personal happiness. On the average, people spend eight hours a day, 40 hours a week, 50 weeks a year at work. With only 24 hours in a day, the largest amount of time will be spent working, getting to work, and talking or thinking about work. Studies show that the leading cause of unhappiness in the United States is job dissatisfaction. With this in mind, why not beat the odds by finding a career that will keep you happy by providing great financial security, diversity, flexibility, prestige, intellectual development, a challenging career, and personal satisfaction?

People who enjoy working with other people and traveling may become sales or field service engineers. People who enjoy life's big picture may become the systems engineers who put all the pieces together. Creative people or people who constantly have new ideas about everything may enjoy working as a design engineer. People who enjoy conducting experiments or working in laboratories may enjoy working as a test engineer.

People who choose engineering can also pursue a career in medicine or law. According to the American Medical Association, biomedical engineers have the highest acceptance rate into medical school over any other undergraduate degree. An individual may also obtain an undergraduate degree in environmental engineering on the way to becoming an attorney specializing in environmental law.

Engineering also lends itself nicely to those entrepreneurial types. Many engineers form construction, environmental, or computer consulting firms because their knowledge is in demand. Some become inventors, and some become teachers or writers. Three engineering students even went on to become the President of the United States!

Many engineers obtain higher degrees in business to become better managers and to receive a broader understanding of the inner workings of engineering companies. Many graduates are working for financial companies writing software programs or constructing financial models to predict Wall Street activities.

An engineering education teaches you how to think through a problem in order to solve it. These mental agility skills will help you solve problems for the rest of your life. The fascinating aspect about problem solving in engineering is that there is almost never a "right" answer. You access several different approaches to solve a problem, and then it is up to you to show everyone how your solution meets the needs of the design.

Let's consider a very elementary example of an systematic problem-solving. You walk into a room and cannot see anything. The room is dark, but the switch is in the "on" position. There are many possible solutions to this problem. Remember that engineers want the best solution. You postulate that the switch could be faulty, the breaker could be flipped, the bulb could be out, the socket could be defective, or the wiring from the switch to the socket could be bad. What would you do first to find the best solution? Most people start with the easiest solution and work to the most difficult. In this case, the easiest solution would be to change the bulb. If that does not solve the problem, you might then check the switch. Are you getting the picture? If the switch is working properly, you would then check the breaker and so on until you discover the cause of the problem.

A bachelor's degree in engineering can lead to a multitude of opportunities. Engineers are on the cutting edge in industry, research, consulting, management, teaching, sales, business, and government. Engineering can require a tremendous amount of time and effort, but, as technology continues to develop, the need for engineers will increase too.

Your Success Depends On You

If you are considering a career in engineering, keep in mind that it will be a lifelong learning experience and everything you do to prepare for it will help you reach your intended goal. The more you expose yourself to the world of engineering, the more opportunities you may have. According to George D. Peterson, the Executive Director of the Accreditation Board for Engineering and Technology (ABET), "employers claim that engineering success today requires more than up-to-the-minute technical capability, it requires the ability to communicate, work in teams, think creatively, learn quickly, and value diversity."

It is important to examine the shape of the career that you want. Identify what kind of career you really want, and try to picture yourself in that role. There are two primary categories that engineers fall into. One shape focuses on doing engineering, and one focuses on applying engineering. For example, do you want to be on the engineering team that designs the next space shuttle, or do you want to be on the space shuttle? Do you want to be the engineer who oversees production in an automobile factory, or do you want to be the expert engineer who gives presentations and answers technical questions on the new specialized suspension of that automobile? There are so many doors open to engineering graduates that this book cannot begin to list them all. See the section on *famous engineers* to glimpse some popular engineers in traditional and non-traditional fields.

You can never begin preparing for this career too soon. Get involved in extracurricular activities that involve math or science. Part-time and or summer jobs also show college admissions departments that you are serious. There are numerous science and engineering camps (see Appendix) available to the motivated student as well as a junior engineering society that offers several ways to get exposure to engineering.

Important Early Preparation

Remember that this book is only one source of information for deciding whether you want to become an engineer. Right now, you need to begin reading everything you can find about engineering and talk to every engineer or engineering student whom you know about the challenges ahead and how to prepare for them. Try attending a summer camp or any programs pertaining to engineering at your school. Obtaining this information now may save you lots of heartache if you decide later that you are on the wrong path.

Academic preparation is also essential to exploring engineering as a career. In addition, getting involved in extracurricular activities pertaining to engineering can give you invaluable exposure. In high school, classes in algebra I and II, trigonometry, biology, physics, calculus, chemistry, computer programming, or computer applications can tell you if you have the aptitude and determination to study engineering. All of the above courses are not required to get into every engineering school, but early preparation can mean the difference between spending four or six years in college. Some universities also require two to three classes in a foreign language for admission. Check into the programs that interest you and begin to fulfill their requirements. Advance Placement or Honors courses are recommended as well as an ACT score of 20 or SAT of 1000.

JUNIOR ENGINEERING TECHNICAL SOCIETY (JETS)

JETS is a national society dedicated to providing students with guidance information about engineering. The Society offers many programs that will help you decide if engineering is the career for you. JETS provides activities, events, competitions, programs, and materials where students can meet engineers and see what they do. Teachers and parents also gain exposure to the social, political, and economic aspects of the impact that engineering can make upon our lives.

JETS offers an academic program called Tests of Engineering Aptitude, Mathematics and Science® (TEAMS) that enables teams of high school students to learn team development and problem-solving skills. TEAMS is the only national competition for pre-engineering students. Students learn how math and science concepts are applied to real-world problems. Teamwork is promoted in an open-book, open-discussion environment, and students often have an engineering mentor.

Past competition problems have included real-world difficulties such as bridge design and rehabilitation, flood analysis, food preservation, solar-powered vehicles, and air transportation. The diversity of the problems shows students the diversity within the engineering field and the diversity of problems that exist in the real world.

Two other programs that are offered by JETS are the National Engineering Design Challenge® (NEDC) and the National Engineering Aptitude Search+® (NEAS+). The NEDC® program is a competition that challenges high school students to design, fabricate, and demonstrate a working solution to a real-world need. The purpose of the NEAS+® program is to help individual students determine their current level of basic engineering skills. Students can determine if additional math, science, or reasoning skills should be acquired.

If JETS interests you, they have an excellent web site at http://www.asee.org/jets/guidance/catalog.html. The site is packed with additional information about the different careers in engineering, programs offered, competitions, activities, and events. They are an excellent resource for obtaining more information about almost any aspect of exploring engineering as a career.

SUMMER CAMPS

Summer camps are another innovative approach for preparing for a career in engineering or evaluating if that career is right for you. Residential and commuter summer engineering camps are offered by numerous universities across the country for high school students and are becoming more popular everyday. Students can develop leadership, professional, and personal organizational skills in addition to meeting and talking with engineers in visits to local engineering companies. Check with the college of engineering at a university near you to see if any summer programs are offered or scan the Engineering Camps Appendix to find a summer program that is right for you.

Universities are not the only place you can find engineering camps; some camps are also offered by industry. The Boeing Company offers an annual *Discover Engineering Summer Science Camp* consisting of two weeks of hands-on science, math, and engineering workshops taught by Boeing engineers. Want to know the best part of all? The camp is free thanks to the thousands of hours volunteered by Boeing engineering and technical support personnel. Call a few of the largest companies in your area and ask about engineering education sponsorship.

FEATURE ARTICLE

Camp Changed Student's View - Involved Engineer Alters Perception, Succeeds in Major

Nancy Fleming was exposed to engineering early on. "My interest in engineering came from my father, who's a quality-control engineer," Fleming, senior in industrial engineering, said.

She also had the chance to learn about engineering in high school through a National Science Foundation engineering camp at Wichita State University. Fleming spent her time at the camp learning about science and research.

"I think before that I had the perception that engineers were male and on the slightly nerdy side," Fleming said. "That camp changed my perception."

Throughout her time at K-State, Fleming has been an active part of the engineering program. During her freshman year, she was recruited by the Society of Women Engineers and has been an active member ever since. Fleming was president the first year she was a senior. "She's one of those people you instantly like," said Ruth Dyer, SWE faculty adviser and associate professor in electrical and computer engineering.

Fleming said people might believe SWE and related organizations are available as a crutch for women engineers. "They're not," she said. "The reason I got in was strictly to meet other women engineers."

Fleming said she hasn't always had such an interest in engineering. "Thinking back to fourth grade, I hated math," she said. In college, Fleming has had to change her perception of herself as an engineer. "I can remember sitting in classes thinking I've got to be the dumbest person here," she said. "Then I started getting good grades in those classes. I had to change my perception."

Fleming has also participated in the Engineering Ambassadors program, the Institute of Industrial Engineering and the Honors Research program. After living in Smurthwaite House for two years, she now serves as the living group's kitchen manager 20 hours a week. She was chosen as an executive member of the Ambassadors her junior year and said she believes the program is much different than the other ambassador programs at K-State. "I had the chance to plan out some goals and objectives for the ambassadors," Fleming said. "We were able to increase visits to high schools by 250%."

In her job at Smurthwaite House, Fleming has had the opportunity to incorporate total quality management into the kitchen situation. She is in charge of the facility and scheduling workers, helps train dietitians and works as a trouble-shooter. "I make sure everyone does their job," she said. As part of the Institute of Industrial Engineers, Fleming was able to present a paper on the inclusion of total quality management at Smurthwaite House during a paper conference hosted by the Institute. Dyer said she's been trying to get Fleming to go to graduate school here. "Nancy has the effect on people where she puts them at ease," Dyer said. "She will definitely be missed."

When she's not presenting papers or working at Smurthwaite House, Fleming said she's looking for a job or trying to squeeze in a little free time. "It doesn't seem like I have any free time. I like to be involved in community service. I'm still involved in Smurthwaite projects, and with SWE's Girl Scout Engineering Day," she said. Fleming said she believes that it's one of the most important things SWE does. "I can see how a direct application of a Girl Scout day like this can influence girls for the better," she said.

Copyright 1995 Student Publications Inc., Kansas State University.

An example camp program is the Mother-Daughter Saturday Academy. It consists of six Saturday morning sessions of experiments, contests, lectures, and demonstrations provided by Cal State L.A. women faculty or students and women engineers working in industry. The program focuses on mechanical, civil, electrical, and manufacturing engineering: the four most common engineering branches. Participants subject a raw egg to a two-story bungee jump, for example, to help girls and mothers understand how engineers test for mechanical properties such as elasticity and toughness (ASEE Prism, Feb 1998). Engineering camp is a highly recommended introduction to the profession.

MATCH YOUR PERSONALITY

Choose a career that matches your personality. Find out as much about yourself as possible by taking personality assessments at career guidance centers and talking to friends, family, guidance counselors, and your math and science teachers. Check the want ads to see what employers are expecting, and contact a local college of engineering to see if it offers tours or has programs for high school students.

There is a primary assessment offered by career placement and counseling centers that may give you some insight into who you are, what conditions you may prefer to work under, and how you think about things, such as the Myers-Briggs type indicator. The test is designed to match your interests with the interests of people who are already in a particular occupation. Some people are ideally suited to be "doers" in engineering, and some are better fits for applying their engineering background to contribute to society in other beneficial ways.

Evaluate your personality closely before you choose a career. Are you an extrovert or an introvert? Do you thrive on change, challenge, consistency, or adversity? Are you a leader, or do you prefer to let someone else lead? Are you willing to work the long hours sometimes associated with a career in engineering? Are you ready for a lifetime of learning? Can you work under pressure, and can you communicate effectively?

Friends and family are also excellent career advisors. Typically, it is very difficult to be objective about your own personality. Friends might see strengths in your character that you never noticed, or they may see weaknesses you hoped they wouldn't notice. Family members may see a "good fit" more easily than you.

Consider things that you have done in the past. What have you enjoyed the most, and what have you found the most frustrating or disliked the most? If someone helped you solve that frustrating problem, would you still dislike it or would you feel as though you rose above the challenge? What does that tell you about yourself?

A word of caution: there is no "right" personality for a career in engineering just as there is no "right" type of engineer. If you have a genuine interest and desire to solve problems, and you are willing to put forth the effort to excel in math and science, then science and engineering have something to offer you. The engineering profession needs all types of engineers and consists of all types of engineers.

The chapters that follow will describe what to expect in college and some of the traditional as well as some of the non traditional paths that are available to engineers. They will also describe several of the major branches of engineering and many of the specialties.

Chapter 2

What Can You Expect in College?

Now that you have decided to pursue an engineering education, you should begin preparing as soon as possible. Scan the appendix of this book, and contact any societies that are of interest to you. Browse their web pages. Ask about their programs to help you prepare for college. Ask to talk to current students participating in programs that are of interest to you. Contact local engineering firms, and ask for a tour. Most firms would be happy to show you around and explain what they do. Several companies encourage continuous improvement in engineering and science education. One such company is ICOS, the world's largest biotechnology firm. They have a summer intern program that allows 10-15 college-level science students a year to work at their facility. They also sponsor a shadow-the-scientist program that brings junior high and high school kids into the labs to see what their researchers are doing.

If you like the company, ask if summer internships are available. Through this simple effort, you have made a contact, and, more importantly, a potential job opportunity may await you when you finish your degree.

Most engineering institutions expect you to have good grades in math, science, English, and social studies. Courses in drafting and computer operation are also helpful. Foreign language classes may be required for admission to some universities. Extracurricular activities will help you gain teamwork and organizational experience.

An extremely valuable engineering tool that is often overlooked is communication skills. Engineers must have good written and verbal communication skills because they often work in teams to design, construct, or analyze problems. Most job postings for engineers require effective written and oral communication skills. The advances in technology over the last ten years have changed the role that engineers play within most companies. In many instances, engineers are the team leaders who manage the technology production by also acquiring business and interpersonal skills.

Choosing the Right School

Choosing the right engineering school for you is as important as wheels are to automobiles. Selecting the right school is a difficult decision that incorporates many of your preferences. Hundreds of schools offer engineering programs, and each school has advantages and disadvantages that are specifically tailored to you personally. Some of the most important considerations for most college-bound students are location, cost, faculty, school size, and academics.

1. Location considerations include distance from home, climate, and the type of industry in the surrounding area. If the surrounding area has industry specific to your degree, opportunities for summer internships, co-op programs, and part-time work experience increase dramatically. Often, these work experience opportunities can lead to jobs after graduation.

2. Cost of attendance is often a critical factor in determining which school to select although your decision should not be based on cost alone. Generally, public institutions are less expensive than private, but there are numerous ways to fund education at any institution. Scholarships are offered through most engineering societies (see the Appendix for popular societies), and the government offers grants and loans. Part-time work, co-op programs, and campus jobs also help reduce the cost of attendance. Check with the financial aid department of the schools you are interested in to see what grants and loans you qualify for. Call the engineering department to check on scholarships offered through the college to incoming students. The

military may also offer opportunities for financing your education. The National Guard is a popular program among college students. The Air Force, Coast Guard, Marines, Merchant Marines, Army, and Navy offer education at reduced cost in exchange for a commitment to serve in the Armed Forces for a certain period of time.

3. Quality faculty is very important for a quality education. A faculty that includes under-represented minorities will broaden your experience and better prepare you to work with a larger diversity of people. Faculty members can bring numerous experiences and expertise to their lectures. Check to make sure that faculty rather than graduate students are teaching the classes. As you proceed to junior-level and senior-level classes, the research of the faculty becomes more important. Check the specialization of each one, and try to select a school that has at least one member actively researching your interests. Finding this affinity allows you a role model. You can talk and learn directly from someone who is interested in the same specialization.

4. School size is important for some students. Large schools offer a greater diversity of people and things to do but often lack the professor-student interaction that small schools can offer. In small schools, you can know a larger percentage of classmates, but in large schools you can meet a much larger number of people. Small is not better than large, and large is not better than small; it is purely a matter of preference.

5. Academics is probably the most important factor in choosing the right school for you. The program should be accredited by the Accreditation Board for Engineering and Technology (ABET). ABET accreditation ensures that the school program follows national standards for faculty, curricula, students, administration, facilities, and institutional commitment. By choosing an ABET program, you are ensured that the faculty has met certain national standards and the program is highly regarded by the profession. Some students like the competitive

atmosphere that accompanies attending a very prestigious school, and some students find they work better in a more relaxed environment. Both types of programs will involve a great deal of studying although some will be more challenging than others. Pick the atmosphere that is closest to your personality and aspirations. Questions you might ask at this point include, do I want to be on the cutting edge of technology? Do I want to find better solutions to existing identifiable problems (even if a current solution already exists)? Or do I want a combination of the two?

Some schools require their students to have computers, and some schools provide computer laboratories. You should check to see if free tutoring is offered through the school and if the professors have posted office hours. Can you email professors questions, and are they answered in a timely fashion? Another consideration is the campus library. Is it easy to find the information you are looking for? Does it have a special engineering library or carry engineering journals?

Students frequently enjoy joining student chapters of professional organizations. These organizations can be an excellent resource in your career search and college experience. Many offer competitions against other colleges. Check to see if a student chapter in the branch of engineering you want to study is offered at the schools you are considering. More details about the specific student chapters and their activities are listed under the different branches of engineering. Some other selection criteria can include sports facilities, leisure activities, community events, cultural events, and campus activity resources.

Accelerated Programs

Some engineering schools are becoming more like professional schools such as law and medicine. This type of school incorporates an undergraduate and graduate degree in which engineering practitioners from industry work on-site to provide clinical training and assistance. Some engineering schools have a five-year combined undergraduate engineering degree/MBA. This duo is attractive to students who want to understand basic management, manufacturing, and large-scale systems engineering and leadership.

Programs are being designed to prepare students for technology decision-making and policy-setting as well as for non-engineering professions. Programs are focusing on broader skills such as written and oral communications, management, economics, and international relations (The Green Report, Engineering Education for a Changing World).

The Successful Student

Once you are in engineering school, there are tools you need to be successful. Engineering is a rigorous and demanding major. Students must be self-disciplined and manage their time effectively. In college courses, the "real" learning often takes place outside the classroom and less time is now spent in the classroom. A general rule of thumb says that, for every hour spent in the classroom, engineering students can expect to spend three hours outside the classroom as compared with two hours for non-technical majors. A good time management system also allows most students to participate in extracurricular activities which broaden experience and are of interest to potential employers.

Engineering curricula vary from school to school; however, most schools don't require you to declare a specific field of interest until the end of your second year. The first two years of engineering school are focused on learning the fundamentals such as chemistry, calculus, physics, and mechanics such as statics and dynamics. Other courses in English, the humanities, and biology are usually required.

The third and fourth years of engineering school are most often spent studying your chosen specialty. Most universities require their students to complete a design project in their senior year. The project is completed in teams or individually and solves a real-world problem. Students can often select a problem they are personally interested in, or local industry may present a problem they are currently exploring. Typically, the project requires a research report and presentation of the design process as well as the results.

Study Smart

Alexander Astin, author of *What Matters in College?: Four Critical Years Revisited,* summarizes that the quality of a student's education is directly related to the student's "involvement." Astin says that successful engineering students need to devote an appropriate amount of time and effort to their studies: Students need to;

1. schedule their study time so that they master the material presented in each class session before the beginning of the next class session;
2. share information frequently with peers and engage in group study and collaborative learning regularly;
3. interact frequently with professors in the classroom and in the professor's office;
4. spend as much time on campus as possible; and
5. get involved in student organizations.

By thinking and preparing now to change your study habits, you can make a big difference in the quality of your education. Free up your commitments when you begin school so you have fewer distractions. Be on the lookout for other people willing to study in groups. Visit your professors regularly, and join the local student chapter of your engineering major. You will feel good about being at the top of your class.

Women and Minorities in Engineering

Engineering was a white male profession until the late 1800s when a few remarkable women and a handful of underrepresented minorities, drawn to the intellectual challenge, joined the ranks. According to a 1993 study conducted by the National Science Foundation, women make up 10% of the current engineering workforce, Asians make up 10%, and underrepresented minorities such as African Americans, Hispanics, and Native Americans make up 6%. A 1996 study, three years later, by the Engineering Workforce Commission stated that 20% of the current engineering students are female. The 1998 junior biomedical engineering class at Louisiana Tech University is 50% female. The increase of successful women into the engineering workforce shows that women also have the aptitude and ambition to be engineers. This diversity will benefit the engineering profession by providing a better representation of society today.

Minorities are very important to the engineering profession. A 1994 ASEE report, titled *Engineering Education for a Changing World*, states "engineering education programs must attract an ethnic and social diversity of students that better reflects the diversity of the U.S. and takes full advantage of the nation's talents. Not only does the engineering profession require a spectrum of skills and backgrounds but it should preserve its historical role as a profession of upward mobility." Different cultures bring new ideas to every table, and the value of such input should be noted.

According to a 1992 study conducted at Carnegie Mellon University, the sophomore chemical engineering class consisted of 35% women and 65% men; civil engineering was 23% women and 77% men; electrical and computer engineering was 7% women and 93% men; mechanical engineering was 8% women and 92% men; and materials science was 6% women and 94% men.

FEATURE ARTICLE

Genius, Not Gender: Recognizing the Contributions of Women Engineers

The number of contributions by women engineers may soon grow rapidly. Soon-to-be published findings from the U.S. Department of Education's Center for Educational Statistics show that in 1974, women received 1.6 percent of all bachelor's degrees in engineering. By 1994, that number had increased by nearly 10-fold, to 14.8 percent. The number of women receiving master's degrees also jumped dramatically, more than doubling between 1984 and 1994. Doctorate degrees in engineering also leaped, with four times as many women earning degrees in 1994 compared to a decade earlier.

The committee's effort is part history lesson, part advocacy. It's important to give women their rightful due for the roles they've played in important inventions, including the cotton gin and reaper, say organizers. Historians now generally agree, they point out, that Eli Whitney and Cyrus McCormick both depended on women for the design of their inventions. Organizers are also committed to continuing the trend of bringing more women to the field of engineering. They note that already there's reason to be optimistic. Besides the progress being made in education, the Society of Women Engineers has grown from a few dozen women who banded together in the early 1950s to more than 15,000 members today, according to Anne Perusek, editor of SWE Magazine. Women engineers also hold an ever-increasing number of positions of authority in private industry, government, and education.

Of course, many large challenges remain, including the need to expand recruitment of women engineers, eliminate vestiges of sexism from the workplace, and actively work to expose new generations of girls and young women to the opportunities available in the field of engineering. There's also a need, the National Engineers Week Committee says, to fill the gaps in the history of engineering to tell the full story of the contributions of women engineers, including:

Ada Byron Lovelace - who collaborated with Charles Babbage, the Englishman credited with inventing the forerunner of the modern computer - wrote a scientific paper in 1843 that anticipated the development of computer software (including the term software), artificial intelligence, and computer music. The U.S. Department of Defense computer language, ADA, is named for her.

Amanda Theodosia Jones invented the vacuum method of food canning, a process that completely changed the entire food processing industry. In a move typical of women inventors of the 19th century, Jones denied the idea came from her inventiveness, but rather from instructions received from her late brother from beyond the grave.

Ellen Swallow Richards pioneered the field of environmental engineering with her groundbreaking research into water contamination. In 1870, she helped conduct the first analysis of Massachussetts' water supply and led the research on two subsequent testings. The work set the standard for the United States and the world. She showed incredible foresight with her insistence that the earth's environment be examined as a whole, rather than in bits and pieces. She also urged tighter controls over solid waste disposal and air, food, and water purity. Ironically, various men who are now known as the Father of Modern Sanitation (Hiram Mills), the first person to study nitrification (Edwin Jordan), and the Father of Public Health (William Sedgwick) all owe substantial credit to Richards. As one historian noted, if they were the fathers...then she was the mother of them all.

At the beginning of the 20th century, **Mary Engle Pennington** revolutionized food delivery with her invention of an insulated train car cooled with ice beds, allowing for the first time the long-distance transportation of perishable food.

After **Mary Anderson** noticed that streetcar drivers had to open the windows of their cars when it rained, she invented the windshield wiper in 1903. By 1916, they were standard equipment on all American cars.

In the 1920's and 1930's, **Beulah Louise Henry** was known as "the Lady Edison" for the many inventions she patented, including a bobbinless lockstitch sewing machine, a doll with bendable arms, a vacuum ice cream freezer, a doll with a radio inside, and a typewriter that made multiple copies without carbon paper. One of the most outstanding features of her career was the way Henry capitalized on her inventions, founding manufacturing companies to produce her creations and making an enormous fortune in the process.

Hedy Lamarr -- the 1940's actress known for her line "Any girl can be glamorous. All you have to do is stand still and look stupid" invented a sophisticated and unique anti-jamming device for use against Nazi radar. While the U.S. War Department rejected her design, years after her patent had expired, Sylvania adapted the design for a device that today speeds satellite communications around the world. Lamarr received neither money, recognition, nor credit.

Grace Murray Hopper, a Rear Admiral in the U.S. Navy, developed the first computer compiler in 1952 and originated the concept that computer programs could be written in English. She once remarked, "No one thought of that earlier because they weren't as lazy as I was." Hopper is also the person who, upon discovering a moth that had jammed the works of an early computer, popularized the term "bug." In 1991, Hopper became the first woman, as an individual, to receive the National Medal of Technology. One of the Navy's newest destroyers -- the U.S.S. Hopper -- is named for her.

Stephanie Kwolek's discovery of a polymade solvent in 1966 led to the production of "Kevlar," the crucial component used in canoe hulls, auto bodies, and perhaps most importantly, bulletproof vests.

Ruth Handler, best known as the inventor of the Barbie doll, also created the first prosthesis for mastectomy patients.

Dr. Bonnie J. Dunbar, who earned a master's degree in ceramic engineering from the University of Washington, worked at Rockwell International in the late 1970s as a senior research engineer, helping to develop the ceramic tiles that enable the space shuttle to survive re-entry. In 1985, she had an opportunity to test those tiles first hand, as an astronaut aboard the shuttle.

The use of semiconductor lasers for communication, CD players, and printers owes much to **Elsa Garmire**, who made tremendous advances in optical devices and quantum electronics that made the commercial use of lasers feasible. Starting with a physics degree from Harvard and a Ph.D. in physics from M.I.T., Garmire went on to discover and explain key features of light scattering and self-focusing, and a host of other phenomena crucial to optical technology. In 1994, she was honored with the Society of Women Engineers Achievement Award.

As part of a 1989 flight on the Space Shuttle Atlantis, **Dr. Mary L. Cleave** was part of a mission team that launched the first planetary probe deployed from a shuttle. She also served as Deputy Project Manager for an ocean color sensor satellite that monitors global marine chlorophyll concentration -- a critical factor in determining the health of the seas. It launched in 1995.

As the first woman to serve on the U.S. Joint Chiefs of Staff, **Dr. Sheila E.**

Widnall has already guaranteed her place in history. But serving since 1993 as the Secretary of the Air Force with responsibility for 380,000 active duty personnel, 251,000 members of the Air National Guard, and 184,000 civilians, and overseeing an annual budget of $62 billion is only the latest in her long list of accomplishments. After graduating from M.I.T. in 1964 with her doctorate in science, Widnall went on to become head of that institution's fluid mechanics division, director of the Fluid Dynamics Research Laboratory and an M.I.T. associate provost. Internationally known for her work in the fluid dynamics of aircraft turbulence and spiraling airflows, Widnall received the Distinguished Service Award from the National Academy of Engineering in 1993, and was inducted into the Women in Aviation Pioneer Hall of Fame in 1996. *Reprinted with the permission of National Engineers Week.*

Statistics indicate that women engineers do not yet receive equal pay for the equal work of their male counterparts. However, women are beginning to accept tenured faculty positions and, in the late 80's to early 90's, the first woman served as dean of an engineering college (Eleanor Baum at the Copper Union). As more women gain positions of leadership within the community, pay scales will also exhibit more of the characteristics of "Genius, Not Gender."

The National Academy of Engineering (NAE) recently launched a new Web site as part of a major effort to encourage young girls and women to choose engineering as a profession. The site highlights the achievements of women engineers and provides information on education, careers, and mentoring.

"The proportion of women entering engineering is significantly lower than those pursuing other scientific disciplines," said NAE President Wm. A. Wulf. "For example, in 1995, 35 percent of all life scientists were women, but only 9 percent of all engineers were women. This website is intended to help young women explore engineering as an exciting and rewarding career opportunity." Check out this outstanding website located at http://www.nae.edu/cwe.

What is a Professional Engineer?

A professional engineer (PE) is an engineer who has been licensed by the state. Just like an attorney needs to pass the bar exam and doctors need to pass the state medical board exam, engineers need to pass the Principles and Practices of Engineering written exam.

Generally, to become a PE, one must graduate from an accredited university, work for four years under the guidance of a professional engineer, and then pass a written test. However, most states offer a pre-registration certificate called the Engineer in Training (EIT) to those who do not yet have four years experience. The EIT certificate is obtained by passing an eight-hour Fundamentals of Engineering (FE) test. Although the certificate does not authorize the practice of engineering, it is the first step of the examination process for full registration. When the engineer gains four years of experience, he or she can then take the second part of the examination that is called Principles and Practices. This test relates specifically to a major branch of engineering.

Although registration is not mandatory, there is a strong trend in the engineering community toward licensure. For example, to be in private practice as a consulting engineer, it is a legal requirement. Many high-level government positions can be filled only by professional engineers, and many states are now requiring instructors at universities to be registered PE's. Most employers expect that students fresh out of college will be well versed in the basics or fundamentals of engineering. The EIT certification merely proves them right. The National Society of Professional Engineers has plenty of information pertaining to the rules and requirements of registration on their website at http://www.nspe.org/.

Chapter 3

Alternatives to Traditional Engineering

Not every engineer craves the traditional engineering path. The opportunities available to the educated non-mainstream engineer are diverse and plentiful. Opportunities such as the Peace Corps, a career in the military, imagineering, inventing, and stunt engineering are only a handful of the possibilities. See the list of famous engineers at the end of this chapter, and learn how they have carved their own niche.

Phillip Condit, CEO of The Boeing Company, is an example of how a degree in engineering can lead individuals into upper management positions. Condit earned a bachelor's degree from University of California at Berkeley, a master's in aeronautical engineering from Princeton, and a master's in management from Massachusetts Institute of Technology.

Condit began working at Boeing 33 years ago. He was head of projects such as the development of the Boeing 757 and 777. The Boeing 777 airplane had 238 teams around the world working simultaneously to produce the first airplane that was 100% digitally designed and preassembled on computer. Boeing employees also develop, manufacture, and support commercial aircraft, space systems, information systems, military aircraft, missiles, and defense-electronics products. Condit, the leader of these 238,000 developers, manufacturers, and support staff, said in an interview with the American Association for Engineering Education, "Students need to know about business economics: What does it cost to build a project? What's involved in integration? Engineering students should be introduced to those subjects so that they are aware of the importance of the costs of their designs."

FEATURE ARTICLE

Engineers: From the Drafting Room to the Board Room

Every year, a new management fad seems to emerge that guarantees success to those who apply it. But, those looking to succeed in the upper levels of management may want to consider a more traditional approach that many of today's top executives have used: a degree in engineering. According to a recent ranking by Business Week of CEOs of the top 1,000 publicly held US companies, more chief executive officers majored in engineering - not marketing, not finance, and not law than any other discipline.

To determine why engineers are "suddenly" leading major corporations, perhaps one first needs to look back in time. In fact, at the height of the industrial revolution in the late 1800s and early 1900s, engineers were much more visible as business leaders. These entrepreneurs such as Thomas Edison, Nikola Tesla, and the Wright brothers, to name a few not only invented new products, but developed the means to produce them. As a result, new corporations were formed to manufacture, market, and distribute their innovations. These organizations were usually led by the engineers who founded them.

Succeeding generations of leadership often possessed many of the characteristics of their founders, including an engineering background.

Today, a second industrial revolution, this one involving communications, is also being led by engineers. Like their predecessors, they are also founding and leading large corporations that are at the forefront of the communications revolution.

Another reason that so many engineers are advancing from the drafting room to the boardroom is that there are so many of them. According to some estimates, there are nearly two million engineers in the United States making it the second-largest profession in the country (behind only teaching). And, as society increasingly requires more technically literate graduates, that figure stands to remain constant, if not increase.

In fact, some may even view an engineering degree much the way law and medical degrees are, as a "marketable skill" that could be applied in a variety of careers, whether industry, academia, or even government. Four current members of the 104th United States Congress have been, or are, registered professional engineers Joe Barton (R-TX), John Hostettler (R-IN), Jay Kim (R-CA), and Lewis Payne (D-VA) and five other Congressmen are engineers by education or experience. In addition, two governors are engineers: Jim Gerringer (Wyoming) and Kirk Fordice (Mississippi). Those of the country's chief executive, the President, three have had engineering backgrounds. Jimmy Carter was a nuclear engineer, Herbert Hoover was a mining engineer, and George

Washington, although not a degreed engineer, is considered one by most historians because of his surveying skills.

Engineers are also well represented in the Wall Street financial community, since most investment banks require not only detailed information on a firm's financial status, but its technical standing as well. Even in established multi-billion dollar corporations, engineers are at the forefront. One just needs to look at a roster of today's top corporations - General Electric (Jack Welch), Xerox (Paul Allaire), Lockheed-Martin (Norm Augustine), Eastman Chemical (Earnest Deavenport), Chevron (Ken Derr), Phillips Petroleum (Wayne Allen), and 3M (Desi DeSimone) are all led by CEOs with engineering degrees. In corporations that produce technical products and services, it's probably to be expected that engineers will lead them into the next millennium; after all, engineers are the ones most familiar with the technical attributes of their products.

Since engineers are the bridge between true science and the benefits received from its application to real problems, they get to remain close to the new and exciting breakthroughs, said John Mihm, vice president of Research and Development (R&D) for Phillips Petroleum Company.

But what about other companies, such as consumer products giants Ben and Jerry's (led by CEO Robert Holland, a mechanical engineer) and Coca-Cola (CEO Roberto Goizueta is a chemical engineering graduate)? Even though the products may not be cutting-edge technology, the processes to deliver them are. Factors such as distribution links, production, R&D, and warehousing all require enormous analytical skills and an understanding of technical processes. The problem-solving skills mastered through an engineering education are often essential in balancing objectives and priorities and developing an action plan. The opportunities to move and work in varied locations also adds greatly to one's ability to see and grasp opportunities, Mihm added. The engineering logic that is part of all engineering also lends itself well to management, with most engineers going from technical expert to project management and on up the management ladder. *Reprinted with the permission of The American Institute of Chemical Engineers.*

Peace Corps

The Peace Corps program was introduced in 1960 by John F. Kennedy at the University of Michigan campus when he was campaigning for the presidency. The Peace Corps offers a peaceful way to work for your country. The purpose of the program is to teach transferable skills that can be used to help people long after you are back at home. Today, Peace Corps volunteers can be found in over 90 countries.

Diversity and adaptability as well as global perspective are all attributes that are sought by employers. The Peace Corps offers the personal experience of living and thinking about the world from a different cultural and environmental perspective. It enables the new engineer to take on more responsibility and obtain more practical experience than a recent college graduate would normally have. For a closer look at an engineer in the Peace Corps, see the article about Charles under environmental engineering.

The Peace Corps offers the opportunity for civil, mechanical, structural, sanitary, architectural, or environmental engineers to train people to develop comprehensive city or town plans; improve water, sanitation, and transportation systems; and construct roads, hospitals, and municipal buildings. Other branches of engineering are also sought to teach math or science classes to school children.

"The toughest job you'll ever love" is the Peace Corps' motto. The adventure begins with eight to twelve weeks of language training most often in your host country. The duration of the stay is two years in which you will gain valuable professional and hands-on experience with all expenses paid.

The resulting readjustment back into the United States gives volunteers a professional edge. They are given first choice for government jobs and currently receive a readjustment allowance for the time spent as a volunteer.

To learn more about The Peace Corps, visit their web site, and read several of the many essays about the experiences of former volunteers.

Military Career

The U.S. Navy has numerous opportunities available to the qualified engineering graduate. As you probably know, the U.S. Navy is a worldwide service consisting of nearly 1 million men and women. The Navy spends billions of dollars on advanced technology, sophisticated equipment, and highly skilled technicians and managers. The mission of the Navy is to maintain the freedom of the seas and protect our interests and those of our allies around the world.

The type and number of officers in the Navy are enormous. Some examples are naval aviators, naval flight officers, nuclear reactor engineers, nuclear power instructors, special operations officers, special warfare officers, submarine warfare officers, aerospace engineering duty officers, cryptology officers, engineering duty officers, oceanography officers, intelligence officers, and public affairs officers.

Navy officers must be college graduates, and the different Navy jobs have different entrance/exit requirements. For example, to become an Aerospace Maintenance Duty Officer (AMDO), the applicant must be between 19 and 29 and is obligated for eight years of military service: four years of active duty and four years in the reserves (inactive duty). To enter the Navy's Nuclear Propulsion Officer Candidate (NUPOC) program, the applicant must be between 19 and 26. Submarine candidates must have normal color vision, serve five years of active duty, and serve three years of inactive duty. NUPOC individuals can receive a college stipend of more than $1400 a month until they graduate and start their officer training. The NUPOC program also offers a special program to engineering students who have completed their sophomore year with a GPA of 3.3 or better in all technical courses.

Following is a list of a few of the many paths which can lead to commission as a Navy officer. Commissioning programs are available for students still in college and for college graduates.

Officer Candidate School (OSC) is a thirteen-week course providing college graduates the initial training to become Navy officers. OSC is an intensive curriculum in naval science and human relations management.

The Nuclear Propulsion Officer Candidate (NUPOC) Program is offered to college juniors and seniors who meet top scholastic requirements and are interested in careers in the nuclear Navy. The program offers monthly pay to the student finishing the final two years of college. Cash bonuses are offered upon acceptance into the program and completion of the Navy's Nuclear Prototype Training.

Aviation Officer Candidate (AOC) and Naval Flight Officer Candidate (NFOC) programs offer college graduates an exciting career in Naval aviation. Upon successful completion of OSC, they are commissioned and attend basic and advanced pilot or naval flight officer training.

The Navy Civil Engineer Corps (CEC) Collegiate Program offers qualified engineering and architecture students in their junior and senior years substantial monthly salaries while completing their civilian education.

The Nuclear Power School Instructor Program and Nuclear Reactor Engineer Program pay qualified college and graduate students approximately $1200 a month while they complete their degrees. Students are required to maintain a GPA of 3.3 or better in all technical courses. Students would not have any active duty service requirements while in college or graduate school.

The Naval Reserve Officer Training Corps (NROTC) program offers tuition and other financial benefits at more than sixty of the country's leading colleges and universities. Two-year and four-year scholarships are also offered, and participants also receive monthly cash allowances.

The United States Naval Academy (USNA) is a four-year undergraduate program that pays a monthly Navy salary. Academy students must be single, not pregnant, with no legal obligation to support a child or children or other individual, and they must serve on active duty for at least six years after graduation.

The Baccalaureate Degree Completion Program (BDCP) is a financial incentive for students to continue their education at accredited four-year colleges or universities. College junior and seniors with excellent scholastic records are eligible. Those students accepted into the program receive monthly pay while completing their degree.

As you can see, there are many ways to become a Navy officer. The Navy can also be viewed as a way to pay for college and receive outstanding training and benefits. The Navy has plenty to offer; stop and talk to a recruiter or call their national information number: 1-800-USA-NAVY.

Experimental Test Pilots and Experimental Test Drivers

Experimental test pilots and experimental test drivers fly or drive new and modified airplanes, automobiles, and motorcycles. Their job is to determine if the planes, automobiles, and motorcycles they test can safely do what they were designed to do before the rest of the world begins to use them.

Manufacturers of transportation vehicles usually send their test pilots and drivers for a year of specialized training. The pilots and drivers usually have a bachelors or masters in engineering, and an operational background flying aircraft or racing cars and motorcycles.

Boeing's chief 777 test pilots are engineers who worked their way into this field by being employed at Boeing or another aircraft company. Other pilots and drivers get involved in pure research, testing new concepts before they're incorporated in new designs.

Test pilots and drivers need to have an adequate knowledge on what makes planes fly the way they do and what makes cars and motorcycles drive the way they do. They must have excellent powers of observation, reason, and persuasion to help ensure that the good designs make it to the public and the bad ones don't.

The Society of Experimental Test Pilots (SETP) has an excellent website at http://www.sept.org/. The site is filled with test pilot experiences, and the flight safety workshops page includes some examples of lessons learned the hard way. If test piloting is interesting to you, don't miss their site.

Imagineering

Have you ever wondered who designed and constructed the theme parks around the world? One trip to DisneyWorld or Disneyland can leave the most reserved of us awestruck and gesturing wildly. Imagineers are responsible for designing all aspects of theme parks. These engineers attempt to merge science and art to create illusion that is so close to reality that your mind can't distinguish if it is real.

Walt Disney opened Disneyland, the first theme park, on July 17th, 1955. Disneyland was different from other amusement parks because amusement parks offered only thrill rides such as roller coasters and water rides. The idea with a theme park was to envelop the visitor in a seemingly different time and place based on stories.

Imagineering, a term coined by Walt Disney, refers to work of the team of people who design theme parks. Part of this team includes illustrators, architects, interior designers, industrial designers, graphic designers, and, of course, engineers. According to Nate Naversen at Imagination Enterprises, "engineers figure out a way to make it work. Whether it be sizing the structural columns and measuring shear forces on a roller coaster, or developing new electronics to make an animatronic character function, engineers do the math to make everything "stand up." Structural and mechanical engineering are the most common majors."

How do they do it? Imagineers attempt to stimulate all five senses; eyes, ears, touch, smell, taste. A sixth sense, imagination, is also stimulated to transport the guest to the magical story world they have created. The more senses that are enveloped simultaneously, the more real the fantasy world appears.

The sense of Imagination is the sixth sense because, without it, the other senses would have less emphasis. Take a look at how each sense is stimulated. A whole team of people may work together to appeal to only one aspect of one sense! For example, the imagineers that manage the visual aspects include the architects, landscapers, and lighting engineers. Imagineers that manage the audio aspects design the music to suggest a mood (can you remember the music in the last scary movie you saw?). There also are imagineers that manage touch, smell, and taste.

Typically, if the story or theme of the attraction can convince people they are in a faraway place or time, the attraction is truly marvelous. Check out Disney's website to find out more about imagineering.

Engineering Invention

Some engineers seem like they are just born inventors. These engineers appear to fall out of the womb with an idea about how to be more efficient or save money. Following are a few examples of companies that were founded by individuals who were trained as engineers. These individuals are creative and know how to stand behind their engineering education. Inventing a product can mean starting your own company or simply selling your idea and design. If you sell your idea and design, you can expect the buying company to pay for the manufacturing and all promotion while you collect a royalty percentage or lump-sum payment. If you start your own company, you will be responsible for manufacturing and marketing your product. The good side of starting your own company is that you will retain all control of your design and make all the money too. The bad side is that you need to come up with "front" money to manufacture your product.

Bungee-Adventures, Inc., is North America's first commercial bungee operation. Two brothers, John and Peter Kockelman, obtained computer and mechanical engineering degrees from Cal Poly San Luis Obispo. The brothers opened Bungee-Adventures, Inc., and have since rigged over 50,000 jumps. Additionally, they wrote the initial draft of the North American Bungee Association Safety Standards. Using engineering skills obtained in college, they have written a computer program that tracks the distance, velocity, acceleration, air-drag, and force of the jumper at any time in the bouncing cycle. The brothers design and manufacture their own bungee cords and are the largest U.S. supplier of cords to the industry.

Bazooka Bubble Gum. Waldo Semon worked as a chemical engineer for B.F. Goodrich Company in Akron, Ohio. Semon was given the job of finding as many uses for rubber as possible. One use for rubber he came up with was bubble gum. "It looked like ordinary gum except that it would blow these great big bubbles. Unfortunately, B.F. Goodrich thought it was a defect and that nobody would buy it," he told the New York Times in 1995. Semon patented the invention in 1931, and, after the patent ran out, Bazooka trademarked the product.

FEATURE ARTICLE

Slinky-The Spring that Captured the Hearts of Millions

How do you turn a simple cold-rolled steel torsion spring into a best-selling toy with more than 250 million sold world-wide? Simply add the imagination of an engineer and the endless ability of children to be amazed and amused by the simplest things. The result, the Slinky, which this year celebrated its 51st anniversary.

The Slinky was the brainchild of mechanical engineer Richard James, a graduate of The Pennsylvania State University. In 1943, while working at a Philadelphia shipyard, James observed a torsion spring bounce off a ship's deck. He foresaw its potential as a children's toy, if he could find the right steel at the right tension. A year later, he succeeded, and the first Slinky, named by his wife Betty, was created.

Since the toy didn't look like much all coiled up, stores were initially reluctant to stock it. In 1945, however, James convinced Gimbel's Department Store in Philadelphia to give him one end of a counter to demonstrate the toy. It was an instant success, and has been delighting children of all ages ever since, including Jim Carrey in the recent movie, Ace Ventura: When Nature Calls.

Betty James explained the toy's success as: It's the simplicity. There are no batteries, no wind up. And, they are reasonably priced. There's something magic about a

Slinky. It sort of comes alive, she said. Indeed, generations of kids have been fascinated by a spring that walks down stairs and slithers from hand to hand. And, adults have rediscovered the toy as a stress reducer. Today, the Slinky is the flagship product of James Industries, Inc., headed since 1960 by Betty James, and headquartered in Hollidaysburg, Pennsylvania. There have been some variations in the product over the years-the Slinky Junior in 1948, the Slinky Dog in 1955 (featured in Disney's, Toy Story), and since 1979, the plastic Slinky-but the basic Slinky has remained unchanged. Between three and four million of the ingeniously simple springs are sold each year for about two dollars each. It remains a part of Americana, on permanent display in the Smithsonian Institution. *Beth G. Shery of the American Institute of Chemical Engineers.*

Famous Engineers

The following is a list of famous people you probably did not know were engineers or had engineering backgrounds!

FEATURE ARTICLE

George Washington - The First U.S. Engineer

A gentleman farmer of inherited wealth and limited formal education, Washington acquired credible surveying skills early in life, but excelled as a manager, strategist, and leader.

Washington directed a growing nation toward technical advancements, invention, and education. He promoted construction of roads, canals, the Capitol, docks and
ports, water works, and new efforts to ex-
tract coal and ores and develop manufacturing resources.

Around the world, technology was
gaining equal footing with pure science.
Washington's contemporaries included James
Watt (Scottish steam-engine inventor); Joseph
Priestley (British chemistry pioneer); Richard Arkwright (British cotton-spinning inventor); John Fitch (American steamboat inventor); and the Montgolfier brothers (French
aeronauts).

First in Washington's heart, it seems,
was agriculture. As a young surveyor, his first
sight of the Shenandoah Valley reportedly in-
spired the vision of an agricultural empire.
As an adult, Washington settled into Mt.
Vernon as a tobacco planter and experimented
with the innovative agricultural techniques
of crop rotation, soil fertilization, and livestock management. He had accurately pre-
dicted the valley's fertile farming potential.

As the foremost American general,
Washington promoted at least one engineering marvel ahead of its time. During the Revo-
lutionary War, he sent David Bushnell's
hand-operated submarine into New York Harbor to sink a British warship. The Turtle's
lone operator attempted to attach a timed
bomb to the British Eagle's hull. The mission failed when the bomb floated away before exploding. The technology just wasn't
advanced enough for Washington's vision,

and submarines didn't become a force in navies for the next 100 years.

On June 9, 1778, at Valley Forge, Pennsylvania, General George Washington issued a call for engineers and engineering education. This order is considered the genesis of a US Army Engineer School, which found its permanent home at Fort Belvoir, Virginia, where Washington had practiced surveying. As President (1789-97), Washington pushed for the passage of the first US Patent Act in 1789, and signed the first official US patent to Samuel Hopkins of Vermont for his process of making potash and pearl ashes. In 1794, President Washington established a Corps of Artillerists and Engineers to be educated and stationed at West Point in New York, which later become the U.S. Military Academy at West Point.

From transportation to education, Washington's engineering vision proved to be ahead of its time. After his death in 1799, many of the technologies he supported provided an impetus to the American Industrial Revolution. New York's Erie Canal (1817-25) was built, and canals soon crisscrossed America east of the Mississippi. By the 1830's, the nation's population tripled, traveling west through canals, along rivers, and across new roads and bridges. The Army Corps of Engineers began many of these projects.

By the middle of the century, the railroads become the favored mode of transportation. As a result, America had gone west and Washington's vision was realized. *Reprinted courtesy of the American Society of Mechanical Engineers.*

Thomas Edison was an inventor in the 1800s. In 1879, he created the first practical incandescent lamp which used carbonized cotton thread that glowed for 40 hours. In 1877, he invented the phonograph, and in 1879 he invented the world's first central electric power station. To this day, he is credited with over 1,000 patents.

Bill Koch was the skipper of America3, the sailboat that beat Italy's I1 Moro boat for the America's Cup in 1992. Koch went on to field the first all-female sailing team to compete for the 1995 Cup.

Koch is the founder of the Oxbow Group, a Florida-based energy holding company which includes over thirty companies interested in electricity production using alternative fuels, coal and petroleum coke trading, oil production, composite pipe manufacturing, and real estate development. Koch received his bachelor's, master's, and doctor of science degrees from Massachusetts Institute of Technology.

Jimmy Carter, the 39th President of the United States, attended Georgia Tech and the U.S. Naval Academy. He served in the navy as an engineer working with nuclear-powered submarines and later retired to manage the family's peanut-farming business.

Alexander Graham Bell invented the telephone.

Herbert Hoover was the 31st President of the United States. He graduated from Stanford University in 1891 with a degree in mining engineering. He went to China and worked for a private corporation as China's leading engineer.

William Hewlett and **David Packard** met as students at Stanford University when they were undergraduates. The two engineering classmates founded Hewlett-Packard in a small garage in 1939. Their first product was a resistance-capacitance audio oscillator based on a design developed by Hewlett in graduate school. They started the multi-billion dollar company with an investment of $538.

Elijah McCoy (1844-1929) was responsible for inventing a lubricator for steam engines. The invention revolutionized the industrial machine industry because it allowed machines to be oiled while still in motion. The term, "real McCoy," refers to his invention that became so popular that people inspecting machines would ask if the machine contained the *real McCoy,* meaning the real thing. Elijah McCoy was educated in mechanical engineering in Scotland and is credited with other inventions such as the ironing board and lawn sprinkler.

Some other famous engineers include **Alfred Hitchcock**, film director of *Psycho* and *The Birds*; **Montel Williams**, author and syndicated talk show host; **Ray Dolby**, founder of Dolby Laboratories; and **Scott Adams**, cartoonist and creator of Dilbert.

Part II

The Many Faces of Engineering

Engineering is a very diverse and challenging field of study. Not all engineering students are alike, and the engineering marketplace is no different. With more than 25 major branches of engineering and 100 specialties, there is something for everyone who pursues the field. Your personal goals, skills, and personality will determine which branch or specialty of engineering is right for you.

The following chapters start out with a major branch of engineering and funnel into the specialized branches within that particular major branch. For example, Chapter 4 focuses on biomedical engineering. Biomedical engineering is the major branch of engineering and biomechanical, biochemical, bioelectrical, clinical, genetic, and rehabilitation engineering are all specialties within this branch. Most often, a student who wants a job in any of the specialties within biomedical engineering, such as clinical or biomechanical, would earn a degree in biomedical engineering and take electives that allow a concentration in clinical or mechanical engineering.

Chapter 4

Biomedical Engineering

The 1997-1998 Milwaukee School of Engineering Average Starting Salary was $40,400.

Biomedical engineering is an exciting field whose objective is to enhance health care by solving complex medical problems with engineering principles. Biomedical engineers want to serve the public, work with health care professionals, and interact with living systems. The field is very broad and allows a large choice of specialties. Many students say they choose biomedical engineering because it is very people-oriented.

Imagine designing a medical device that appears to breath life into someone. The inventors of the pacemaker were biomedical engineers who literally gave individuals the ability to do physical activities such as walking up a flight of stairs or walking around the block.

The biomedical engineering field changes very rapidly. New technology is being designed and fabricated every day. Biomedical engineers can expect a very satisfying career with tremendous diversity and growth potential. Some specialty branches of biomedical engineering are biomechanical, bioelectrical, biochemical, rehabilitation, clinical, and genetic engineering. There are also many sub-specialties within biomedical engineering such as surgical lasers, telemedicine, nuclear medicine, and clinical computer systems.

BIOMECHANICAL ENGINEERING

Biomechanical engineering is the specialty that sees the human body as a mechanical structure. These specialists investigate the stresses on bones and muscles. They might work for a company such as Nike to design a new running shoe after studying the impact that is caused by running. Biomechanical engineers may also design artificial limbs, joint replacements, or new materials to replace ligaments, tendons, or bone. An early development from a biomechanical engineer was the invention of the iron lung which was an airtight respirator consisting of a metal tank that enclosed the entire body except for the head. It provided artificial respiration by contracting and expanding the walls of the chest.

A fascinating application of biomechanical engineering according to Ellen Morrissey and Donald Lehr of the Nolan/Lehr Group is the helmets of hockey players. "Though they appear to be made of a single piece of material, they are actually three different parts fitted together in an intricate geometric configuration refined over the years for maximum energy absorption." (To test the helmet's ability to attenuate impacts, manufacturers fit helmets with instrumental test heads and then drop them several meters. At the end of the drop, known as a "sudden deceleration," the testers examine the helmet's level of protection and whether it has withstood impacts from 275 to 300 G-forces.) Besides protection, the helmet must also be light enough to keep the head cool, since hockey players are in constant rotation and release a great deal of heat through their head. Further, the lightness is important to allow the player to accelerate at high speeds and then, since the sudden stops of the player square the effect of inertia, stop without tumbling off balance.

BIOELECTRICAL ENGINEERING

Bioelectrical engineers may work in the research and development department of a medical equipment manufacturer developing hospital equipment or other devices to diagnose or treat disease. They may provide training for doctors and nurses on the effective use of such equipment and maintain the equipment as a field or customer engineer. Bioelectrical inventions are everywhere, from the digital ear thermometer to the very sophisticated MRI machines. Another bioelectrical development is the pacemaker which is a device that senses irregular or arrested heart rhythms and restores the rhythms by giving electrical stimulation to the heart muscle. Bioelectrical engineers have also developed the electrocardiogram machine which records, through electrodes placed on the skin, the beating of a heart. The bioelectrical engineer may design software or devices to aid doctors and hospitals such as electrophysiology cardiac monitors or telemedicine equipment. They may design devices to aid patients to self-monitor their conditions successfully, or they may help a paraplegic become self-sufficient by designing an electrical system to regulate all switches and or appliances in the patient's house.

BIOCHEMICAL ENGINEERING

Biochemical engineers concern themselves with body responses on a microscopic level. These engineers study the interactions between artificial materials that may cause negative reactions in the human body. Biochemical engineers apply anatomy, biochemistry, and cellular mechanics to understand diseases and modes of intervention. Biochemical engineers developed woven acrylic artificial arteries to prevent blood clotting in artificial blood vessels. Biochemical engineers also designed and constructed the artificial kidney for patients with incurable kidney disease.

REHABILITATION ENGINEERING

Rehabilitation engineering is a very popular specialty within biomedical engineering. Rehabilitation engineers participate in the research and development of assistive technology for individuals with disabilities. According to the Biomedical Engineering Society, "rehabilitation engineers enhance the capabilities and improve the quality of life for individuals with physical and cognitive impairments."

Assistive technology includes devices such as powered wheelchairs, talking computers, hearing aids, electronic talking devices, and any facilities that are modified, including grab bars for showers and restrooms. Recreational assistive technology such as specially adapted skis and fishing poles are also available. If rehabilitation engineering interests you, watch the special Olympics to get a feeling for the assortment of assistive technology devices available and the feeling of power and accomplishment that is associated with giving a handicapped person a new lease on life, providing a way to meet everyday life challenges successfully, and eliminating some of the challenges associated with having a disability in today's society.

A rehabilitation engineer may travel to a patient who was recently in an accident leaving him or her in a wheelchair. The engineer could redesign the patient's work space to include such changes as a desk to raise and lower at the push of a button, wider doorways, and ramps inside the house to accommodate a wheelchair. A rehabilitation engineer may also redesign computer systems to assist people with cognitive or physical disabilities. One rehabilitation engineer put Braille letters on a keyboard so blind people could type. Another rehabilitation engineer developed a system so people with no feeling below the waist could drive an automobile.

CLINICAL ENGINEERING

Clinical engineering is the branch of biomedical engineering that applies technology to health care in organizations such as hospitals and long-term care facilities and for medical equipment vendors. Clinical engineers must understand the relationship of the equipment to the diagnosis, care, and treatment of the patient. High-risk assessments and the development of maintenance schedules and protocols are some of the other tasks they perform. They may also provide training for doctors, nurses, and other health professionals on the effective use of all medical equipment, and they may maintain the equipment. Clinical engineers may also evaluate equipment prior to purchase, safety test the equipment, or modify existing hospital equipment. Often, they may also participate in accident/incident investigations.

Visit the website of the American Society for Healthcare Engineering (ASHE) at http://www.ashe.org/ to find out more about clinical engineering and the field of healthcare design, construction, and safety.

GENETIC ENGINEERING

Genetic engineering is very new branch of biomedical engineering which researches ways to manipulate DNA. Many people have negative responses to genetic engineering because of the ethical and legal issues that surround the replication of DNA. However, genetic engineers have also engineered products to break down oil slicks efficiently, and they have engineered new plants that are resistant to diseases or insects.

As you can see, the biomedical engineering field is extremely diverse and a very real way to make a very large impact on society. Biomedical engineers work in hospitals, government regulatory agencies, corporations, medical device companies, research labs, and universities. Many go to medical school because biomedical engineers have the highest acceptance rate into medical school than people with any other degree. Many go to law school and become patent attorneys or regulatory requirement attorneys. Some go into teaching, and many become consultants or advisers to medical companies.

The Biomedical Engineering Society (BMES) has an excellent web site at http://mecca.mecca.org/BME/BMES/society/about.html that details the numerous specialties available within biomedical engineering and provides links for many additional information resources such as job opportunities, individual state BMES chapters, and prominent companies in the medical industry.

Chapter 5

Chemical Engineering

According to the 1998 AIChE Salary Survey, the median salary for '97 chemical engineering graduates with a bachelor's degree was $43,000.

Chemical engineers are creative, innovative problem-solvers who enjoy great diversity in their field. Chemical engineering is very intellectually challenging and offers one of the highest starting salaries of all the engineering disciplines. Everything that our senses enjoy is made up of chemicals in one way or another. Chemical engineers have worked on creating the purple rose that has no thorns, the caramel on a caramel apple, and even your tennis shoes. The chemical engineering profession has improved water and waste systems, created new drugs and drug delivery systems, and improved the crop yields for farmers, just to name a few of the challenges.

Chemical engineers enjoy being able to choose from many specialties within their discipline. A chemical engineering student who picks a track in environmental engineering might be interested in helping reduce pollution or producing better food. A chemical engineer with a track in biomedical engineering is often called a biochemical engineer and may design new or improved artificial organs. If you are more attracted to the big picture, you might see yourself looking for ways to streamline processes or increase safety with a specialty as a process design engineer.

Traditionally, chemical, petroleum, and pharmaceutical companies employed the bulk of the chemical engineering profession. Pharmaceutical companies employ a large number of chemical engineers to research, develop, or design their product lines. However, many are now also employed in biotechnology, material science (such as the plastics, rubber, ceramics, and metals industries), and electronics. The food industry, the Department of Energy, and the Environmental Protection Agency have also become prominent employers.

Many chemicals engineers have opted for careers in research. A chemical engineer who goes to medical school could become a medical doctor specializing in rare diseases or a medical researcher. A chemical engineer who goes to law school could be a patent attorney or simply a specialized attorney for a company that has invented a new drug or drug delivery system.

The American Institute of Chemical Engineers (AIChE) offers a student chapter to help the student step gracefully into the real world of chemical engineering. Thousands of students across the nation participate in the organization at more than 150 campus locations. The organization is very supportive of students and encourages growth by offering numerous scholarships, competitions, and awards. Visit their web site at: http://www.aiche.org/ (also listed in the Appendix), and see for yourself all the benefits of being a member of this very helpful and supportive society. The site is packed with information, has profiles of what many chemical engineers are doing on a daily basis, and gives very realistic career information. Those of you seriously interested in chemical engineering should not miss this challenging career!

BIOCHEMICAL ENGINEERING

Biochemical engineers concern themselves with body responses on a microscopic level. These engineers study the interactions between artificial materials that may cause negative reactions in the human body. Biochemical engineers apply anatomy, biochemistry, and cellular mechanics to understand diseases and modes of intervention. Biochemical engineers developed woven acrylic artificial arteries to prevent blood clotting in artificial blood vessels. Biochemical engineers also designed and constructed the artificial kidney for patients with incurable kidney disease.

FOOD ENGINEERING

Food engineers are involved in all aspects of food preparation and processing. From a candy bar to supermarket freezer foods, food engineers have influenced packaging, storage, and distribution systems. There is a large demand for engineers within the food industry. New products and environmentally friendly food-processing equipment need to be developed.

Food engineering is a branch of chemical engineering that pertains to the properties and characteristics of foods that affect their processing. Food engineering requires an understanding of the chemical, biochemical, microbiological, and physical characteristics of food. There will be a shortage of food engineers as long as society demands that engineers develop lower-fat, lower-salt, lower-cholesterol, or nutrient-packed foods for their diets.

FEATURE ARTICLE

Food for Thought - The Engineer Who Came to Dinner

Remember when the frozen "TV dinner" was the only convenience food around? If you do, it's not so much a reflection of your age, as of the rapid changes in food technology. Whether they're more convenient, tastier, fresher, more nutritious, or just more fun, many of today's foods are engineering achievements.

What do engineers have to do with food? The question might actually be, what don't they? According to most reports, agriculture and food processing account for 20 percent of the nation's gross national product. Many of the 1.8 million engineers in the country work on getting food to your table every day, as well as on special things like Valentine's Day chocolates and food for astronauts on the Space Shuttle.

Of course, a food engineer's most important job is to ensure food safety, supply, nutrition, and stability. But, beyond these basics, engineers continue to work to make food tastier, more convenient, and more appealing.

While TV dinners, now 42 years old, may not inspire the excitement they once did, even some recent innovations are pretty much taken for granted. One example is TetraPak juice boxes, which combine added convenience with improved product quality and stability.

Recently, with concerns about landfill capacity, engineers have looked more closely at how to make food packaging more environmentally friendly.

Everyone's familiar with decaffeinated coffee. Yet how many realize that engineers developed the supercritical carbon dioxide process to remove caffeine from coffee without using traditional hydrocarbon solvents? Now, we can all sleep better.

And, what about the ubiquitous microwave and microwavable food, not to mention freeze-dried and dehydrated foods, boil in a bag, and all the other forms of food packaging? All were developed by engineers.

To wash all this food down, you might drink milk bought right off the grocery shelf, without refrigeration. Using ultra-high temperature processing, engineers have developed a way to keep milk fresh longer, even at room temperature. Of course, this is just the latest development in a series of engineered advances for milk that includes vitamin fortification and lactose-free and low-fat varieties.

For dessert, how about some engineered ice cream? Frozen desserts, like ice cream, have presented unique challenges to engineers. Ice cream is a three-phase emulsion system (oil, water, and air) which has to be delicately balanced to provide the desired product characteristics.

Processing conditions such as freezing rate influence the rate of ice crystal formation and have an effect on the resulting texture and "mouthfeel" of the product. Formulation plays a role as well, when different flavors, fruits, and colors are added, the balance of the system is altered.

Food provides a special challenge to engineers, because it is not as simple as other systems where physical and chemical properties are well defined and compositions known. Most foods are complex mixtures made up of thousands of compounds. Although food's chemical components can be broadly categorized as proteins, carbohydrates, fats, vitamins, minerals, flavors, and enzymes, this simplification does not truly reflect the variety of compounds within each class.

What complicates matters more is that the compounds all interact with each other. And, processing food in the plant or cooking it at home changes the flavor, color, and nutritional characteristics.

Food engineers are also involved in cutting-edge technologies, like genetic engineering, to produce crops more resistant to pests, or more durable for processing. In processing, newer technologies such as freeze drying or supercritical extraction are used in cases where maintaining heat-liable compounds (such as flavors) are important.

How is a typical new food "engineered?" After a product concept is developed in a lab, it is done "bench-scale," where there is close control of composition and processing. One of the engineer's tasks is to translate a lab process to large-scale production. The product also has to be packaged in a way to ensure easy distribution and preparation. And, through the entire interval, from the time the product leaves the plant until it is served at the table, it must maintain its quality.

Established products must be continually "re-engineered" to give them advantages over the competition. These include better overall flavor (or more variety), making the packaging more recyclable, reducing manufacturing costs, improving nutrition, or innovations for added convenience. *Reprinted courtesy of The American Institute of Chemical Engineers.*

MATERIALS ENGINEERING

Materials engineers design, fabricate and test materials. They may be involved with making automobiles lighter and more fuel efficient by creating stronger and lighter metals. They may be involved with creating new knees and elbows using special polymers, or they may be designing new materials for the next space shuttle.

A materials engineer can work with any type of material such as plastic, wood, ceramic, petroleum, or metals and create completely new synthetic products by rearranging their molecular structure. For example, Teflon (polytetrafluoroethylene), the product that coats millions of cooking pans, was invented by freezing and compressing a gas related to refrigerants.

There are numerous opportunities available to materials engineers. Materials can lead to a career in the transportation industry making cars, trains, boats, and buses run more fuel efficiently. Special lubrication products can be designed for race car suspensions and high-strength alloys for space travel. Materials engineering can also lead to a career in communications. Semiconductor companies employ materials engineers to develop silicone to speed up computers by allowing faster transport of electronic signals. New and purer forms of germanium, cesium, tungsten, and copper that are used in electronic components also need to be developed to lower the cost and increase the stability of all electronic components and systems.

More information about materials engineering can be found atthe Society for Biomaterials website at http://www.biomaterials.org/, the Materials Engineering and Sciences Division of the AIChE at http://www.aiche.org/,the Materials Engineering Division of the ASCE at http://www.asce.org/, and the Materials Division of the ASME at http://www.asme.org/.

Chapter 6

Civil Engineering

Entry-level engineers earn an average of $32,000, according to the ASCE 1995 Salary Survey.

Civil engineering is one of the oldest and largest branches of engineering. Traditionally, civil engineers plan and design such things as roads, bridges, high-rises, dams, and airports just to name a few. However, population growth and a booming economy will have the civil engineer designing new things such as underwater tunnels, new and better wastewater treatment plants, solutions for highway congestion, and special tracks for the magnetic levitation trains of the future. As our current understanding of technology continues to increase, the demand for the diverse talents of a civil engineer will increase too.

Money magazine ranked civil engineering the 10th highest paying profession, and the fifth "best job" in America out of 100 based on salary, prestige, growth, and security in 1994.

Civil engineers enjoy being able to choose from many specialties within their discipline. A student who picks a track in environmental engineering might be interested in monitoring air pollution or transforming wetlands into golf courses. A student who picks a track in structural engineering might be interested in working to make buildings and or roads earthquake safe. This structural engineering student may also design offshore oil rigs or even a coliseum which hosts sporting events and concerts. With an emphasis in transportation engineering, the student will design the transportation of the future. That may include working with high-speed trains or new types of boats. There is no limit to the versatility and opportunity of the civil engineering profession.

Approximately 60% of civil engineers work in construction, transportation, manufacturing, and utilities. Most of the remaining 40% work for federal, state, or local government agencies. Almost half of these governmental jobs involve developing designs as engineering consultants.

Some civil engineers have opted for a career in research where they may attempt to find newer, stronger, more resilient materials. A civil engineer who goes to law school could be an earthquake or hurricane insurance attorney or simply a specialized attorney for a major construction company.

The American Society of Civil Engineers (ASCE) offers a student chapter to help the student step easily into the real world of civil engineering. The organization boasts 15,000 student members across the nation. ASCE is very supportive of students and encourages growth by offering numerous scholarships, competitions, and awards to its students. One of the favorite annual competitions is designing and building a concrete canoe. The seniors of sixteen teams design, construct, and race a concrete canoe. Each boat is judged on its design, workmanship, presentation, and actual performance. Visit the ASCE web site at: http://www.asce.org/ (also listed in the Appendix). Being a member of the ASCE includes such benefits as salary information, professional recommendations, Job Bank USA at a discount, and numerous scholarships.

ARCHITECTURAL ENGINEERING

Architectural engineering, according to the National Society of Architectural Engineers (NSAE), is "the application of engineering principles to the design of technical systems of buildings."

Do you have the ability to be analytical as well as creative? Can you think systematically and pragmatically, and then turn around and be creative and spontaneous? If so, architectural engineering may be for you. Architectural engineers need to be aesthetic as well as technical, creative as well as rational. They need to know if what looks good on paper is also technically possible.

Architectural engineers may specialize in the building's structure. In this specialty, the engineer accommodates hurricane wind, snow, or earthquake forces. Another specialty is the building's mechanical system. This specialist is concerned with regulating the air flow in buildings, deciding on thickness of walls, materials, heat sources inside and outside of the building, plumbing, heating, and air conditioning. The electrical and lighting system specialist is responsible for distributing electricity throughout the building, and some architectural engineers specialize in managing construction projects. These individuals focus on safety, cost, and construction methods of designing a building.

The World Wide Web virtual library on architectural engineering has an excellent web site at http://energy.arce.ukans.edu/wwwvl/whatarce. The site gives an excellent description of architectural engineering as well as an example of how many architectural engineers worked together to create the $51 million New Jersey State Aquarium. The site gives information on the greatest architectural engineers of all time and has essays from other students about what the future holds for building technology.

Currently, there are only thirteen accredited architectural engineering programs in the United States. Check out the NSAE web site at http://energy.arce.ukans.edu/nsae/main.html for more information on this exciting branch of engineering.

ENVIRONMENTAL ENGINEERING

Environmental engineering, often called sanitary engineering before 1970, is focused on the development of water distribution systems, recycling methods, sewage treatment plants, and pollution and pesticide prevention. The field is growing very quickly and offers a challenging and satisfying chance to protect the health and safety of people and our environment. These earth-friendly professionals concern themselves with preventing and fixing problems caused by industrialization. They concentrate on delivering better environmental conditions for the public.

Many large firms employ environmental engineers to decide how to dispose of toxic material and or to control toxic emissions. Some environmental engineers work for the government inspecting pollution control systems, and some environmental engineers work designing or inspecting water treatment systems. Environmental engineers also develop and administer the regulations that protect health, safety, and the environment.

The Footsteps of an Environmental Engineer

After Charles graduated from high school, he attended the University of Wyoming to study civil engineering. His father had an engineering degree, and it seemed like a logical choice for Charles since he was good at math and science. "Besides" he said, "I knew that I really wanted to work with water."

When Charles finished his bachelor's degree, he joined the Peace Corps and was sent to East Africa. "I had always been interested in the Peace Corps and it gave me a chance to travel and do something worthwhile with my education. During the first year, Charles worked on a small pipeline project to supply water to a community in the area he lived. During his second year, Charles worked with small groups of women training them to build concrete water tanks to catch and store rain water.

Charles' time in Africa with the Peace Corps increased his interest in water and in engineering. He decided to return to school to get a master's degree in environmental engineering at Clemson University.

Today, Charles works for a consulting environmental engineering firm. He is primarily involved in work related with the expansion of municipal wastewater treatment facilities. Expansion of the treatment plants is required to ensure adequate capacity for future growth of the communities and to ensure that water quality standards as set by state and federal agencies are met. Typical projects involve millions of dollars and may take two years or more to complete.

More information, such as "Innovations in Environmental Engineering" and numerous articles from the *Environmental Engineer* magazine, can be found at the American Academy of Environmental Engineers (AAEE) web site: http://www.enviro-engrs.org/.

STRUCTURAL ENGINEERING

Structural engineering is a very diverse career with numerous opportunities. Structural engineering not only focuses on the design and development of structures such as houses, coliseums, bridges, and shopping malls but also focuses on the design and development of materials that will create these structures. The structural engineering profession offers exciting challenges and potential for growth. New and more sophisticated materials are being produced every day that will change the shape and future of structures.

The structural engineer must be creative and resourceful. This engineer needs to be able to visualize the framework of a structure and determine what forces will produce what loads upon it. Many structural engineers are employed in California designing buildings that are able to sustain ground-shaking (earthquake) loads.

Structural engineers may work as governmental building inspectors, as designers, or as construction consultants for architectural and construction firms. Some consult on building renovation or research ways to develop new and stronger materials. The challenge in structural engineering is not just designing and developing the best and safest structure, but designing and developing new ways to test, remodel, or construct structures inexpensively without compromising safety or personal integrity. For more information, visit the Structural Engineering Institute(SEI) of the ASCE website at http://www.asce.org/sei/index.html.

TRANSPORTATION ENGINEERING

Transportation engineering is a branch of civil engineering whose goal is to allow people and goods to move safely, rapidly, conveniently, and efficiently. Transportation engineers design streets, highways, and public transportation systems. They design parking lots and traffic flow patterns that will prevent major congestion at busy intersections, shopping malls, and sporting events. They are involved in planning and designing airports, railroads, and even busy pedestrian thoroughfares.

Transportation engineering is an exciting field that will see increased demand over the next ten years. Whether you like to work indoors or outdoors, transportation engineering has something for you.

You can create computer models of new shopping centers and universities or work outside solving on-site construction problems.

Imagine being an expert witness in a court of law because you designed a specific transportation system. Many transportation engineers are private consultants or involved in research. Federal, state, and local agencies also employ an abundance of transportation engineers. The Institute of Transportation Engineers (ITE) has an informative web site at http://www.ite.org/. If you are seriously interested in transportation engineering, this site has numerous examples and information resources.

Chapter 7

Electrical Engineering

According to the July 1998 National Association of Colleges and Employers (formerly the College Placement Council) report, the average starting salary offers were $42,931.

Electrical and electronic engineering is very diverse and progressive. The field has grown very rapidly and employs 370,000 engineers, making it the largest branch of engineering. Electrical engineers are imaginative problem-solvers. They enjoy challenges.

Electrical and electronic engineers design, develop, test, and manufacture electrical and electronic equipment. The developments of elecronic engineers are everywhere. There are thousands of electrical devices and systems available today that electrical engineers have somehow touched. Anything you plug into the wall such as stereos, computers, microwaves, televisions, power tools, air-conditioners, and major appliances just to name a few has been touched by an electrical engineer. Even things you can't plug into the wall such as satellites, cellular phones, and beepers have been designed, manufactured, or modified by electrical engineers.

Major specializations within electrical engineering include power plant work, communications, and computer engineering. Some of the electrical engineers who specialize in power applications work for utility companies designing power distribution systems. Some with this specialization work on generating electricity by utilizing alternative energy sources.

Communications is also a large field within electrical engineering. Just think about the amazing information superhighway (Internet). Millions and millions of people connect simultaneously to the vast network of information. It won't be long before the Internet is a standard in every household just as televisions are now. Communications specialists also try to improve radio signals, television, and telephone connections. As a communications specialist, you may design a very fast and affordable video phone.

The Institute of Electrical and Electronic Engineering (IEEE) has a fantastic web site at http://engine.ieee.org/ that is jam-packed with information about the world of electrical engineering. See the numerous branches within the world's largest technical professional society. The web site has pages on internships and scholarships. It lists information on job hunting and has a job bank. Twenty-five percent of the world's technical papers are produced each year through the IEEE. The Institute has student chapters at numerous universities and offers student benefits such as group insurance programs, credit cards, auto and education loans, Kinko's copy service discounts, and car rental discounts. Student receive the IEEE SPECTRUM magazine and a discount on membership. The web site is well worth the time invested in browsing.

FEATURE ARTICLE

Magnetic Tape Recording

You probably never saw Marvin Camras on the evening news. Nor did you hear his voice booming from the stereo. Chances are, you didn't even spot his name on a credit card or an American Express commercial. Camras was no media superstar, yet he was the man who made possible today's

$5-billion electronic communications industry. That's because he developed magnetic tape recording, the technology behind audio cassettes, videotape, computer floppy disks, and even credit card magnetic strips.

Camras developed an interest in electronics while a youngster growing up in Chicago. At age 18, to help his cousin practice singing, he first recorded sound on magnetically-charged piano wires. Shortly thereafter, Camras discovered that using magnetic tape eased the work of splicing and storing the recordings. His patent on the process was licensed to General Electric in the mid-1930s, and within a few years, 130 companies around the globe were using his inventions to manufacture recording devices.

Camras studied engineering at what is now the Illinois Institute of Technology, where he is still on the faculty as a research professor. While an undergraduate, he was invited by his professors to refine his discoveries as part of the staff of the school's research foundation.

During World War II, Camras pursued military applications of the magnetic recorder, developing the famed "Model 50," a portable machine that the Allies used to play recorded, amplified battle sounds at decoy locations during the Normandy invasion. His wartime patents of a ferric oxide magnetic tape, and a method for reducing noise and distortion by using high-frequency bias, are still standards in consumer tape recorders.

In 1950, Camras unveiled a prototype videotape recorder, which led to the widespread use of videotape, the end of live television, and the eventual development of the videocassette recorder now found in most American homes. He received more than 500 patents, which have been licensed to over 100 manufacturers worldwide. His many honors included induction into the Inventors Hall of Fame in 1985, and the National Medal of Technology in 1990. *Christopher Currie, IEEE-USA.*

COMPUTER ENGINEERING

Computer engineering deals with the many aspects of computer systems. It is a rapidly growing field full of exciting and diverse opportunities. These engineers may design computer systems, networks, operating systems, or software. They may design the future automobile dashboard computers that will monitor engine functions.

Many computer engineers are employed by large corporations helping employees with hardware or software problems. They may install networks within companies and develop in-house software programs.

Computer engineers may also work in research and development. Talking computers, video phones, and voice-activated automobiles are all in the near future. To get these inventions to market, someone needs to research and develop them. For more information visit the IEEE Computer Society at http://www.ieee.org/society/ce.html

SOFTWARE ENGINEERING

Software engineering is on the cutting edge of technology. Since the world is becoming more computerized, software engineering is becoming one of the most demanding and progressive fields of engineering available. Software enables us to use computers. It is the translator between humans and computers. Without software, a computer would be nothing but ones and zeros.

The current demand for software engineers far exceeds the supply available. Some of the largest employers of software engineers include Microsoft, Motorola, Autodesk, Netscape, Adobe, Symantec, Nintendo, and Corel. This list is by no means exhaustive. To find more employers, simply look at who makes the software on any computer. There are thousands of software manufacturers that hire software engineers.

To prepare for a career in software engineering, one needs to gain exposure to as many programming languages as possible. Popular job requirements are C/C++, Unix, OLE, Pearl, Java, HTML, CGI Coding, Windows 95, or Window NT. Go to the websites of the popular software engineer employers and check out their job postings to keep current with the inevitable rapid changes this industry will witness. Visit the website of the Software Engineering Institiute at http://www.sei.cmu.edu/.

OPTICAL ENGINEERING

Optical engineering is a progressive and exciting new field. Optical engineers design and develop devices and measurement systems such as lasers and fiber optics that utilize the properties of light.

Lasers are used in many different kinds of applications. Medical doctors use lasers to cut out birthmarks and cancerous growths. They fix detached retinas, cauterize wounds, and vaporize kidney stones. Your home and car CD players use laser light to play your favorite music. Laser printers and supermarket scanners are other examples of how laser technology has merged into our lives.

Fiber optics is also another expanding branch of optical engineering. Fiber optics are hair-sized strands of glass that carry voice and video information over long distances in the form of pulses of light. Fiber optic systems run all over the world. They run across the country and even underwater to neighboring countries.

Optical engineers of the future may design new virtual reality games or air-combat simulators. They may seek to optimize CD storage capacity or develop new medical applications such as telemedicine. They may focus on making the Internet faster and more accessible.

Chapter 8

Mechanical Engineering

According to the National Association of Colleges and Employers, mechanical engineering graduates command the 6th highest salaries out of college:$38,113

Mechanical engineers are the wheels of the world. This type of engineering is the broadest and most diverse engineering discipline. Not many people can perform their jobs without mechanical engineers. The creations of mechanical engineers impact all of us. Mechanical engineers design, develop, and manufacture every kind of vehicle, power system, machine, and tool. Any type of machine that produces, transmits, or uses power is most likely the product of a mechanical engineer. There is hardly any aspect of life that has not been influenced by a mechanical engineer.

The best way to describe this field is to give you an inside look at the many student design competitions that are sponsored or co-sponsored by the American Society of Mechanical Engineers (ASME). These competitions are developed to encourage and motivate students. The competition focuses on teamwork and allows the students to get a feeling of the design process, cost of materials, and team environment.

84 Is There an Engineer Inside You?

1997 Propane Vehicle Challenge. In this competition, seventeen university teams met in Texas with trucks and minivans that had been converted to run on propane instead of gasoline. The vehicles raced and were subjected to emissions, fuel, and economy tests.

Racing Solar Cars. This competition was a grueling ten-day, 1240-mile solar power car biennial race that began at the Indianapolis 500 speedway and ended in Colorado Springs, Colorado. Several schools created environmentally friendly solar-powered cars while concentrating on designs that would make the cars faster, lighter, and more efficient.

Human-Powered Vehicle Competition. This competition consisted of three vehicle divisions in three different events lasting for three days. The divisions were tandem, single-rider, and practical. The three events were presentation, sprint, and endurance. Several schools met at the University of California at San Diego for this competition with the vehicles they had designed and constructed.

Although these examples of competitions are informative, they are by no means the only projects mechanical engineering students are involved in. Hopefully, these competitions have given you some insight into the future of mechanical engineering and some of the challenges you may be facing.

Mechanical engineers also design and develop jet engines, steam engines, power plants, underwater structures, hydraulic systems, and measurement devices, just to name a few. They can work in testing or product maintenance.

Stephen Katsaros, a mechanical engineering student from Purdue with an entrepreneurial spirit decided to develop his own inventions. Katsaros has developed a tool for sharpening alpine skis, a bicycle overhead storage system (BOSS), and, through his creativity and mechanical advantage, is at work on several other projects. The surprising lesson Katsaros reveals is that "college is the best time an individual has to start a business because of all the available resources: the professors, the students to bounce ideas off of, the computers, and at Purdue we had a full machine shop." To hear more about this innovative student and his struggle to become an inventor, go to his web page at http://www.asme.org/students/mech_adv/entrep.htm.

The ASME web site is packed with excellent information for students. The Society produces a student magazine called *The Mechanical Advantage* that tells about the competitions, scholarships, industry news, grant programs, and job market forecasts. If you are interested in mechanical engineering, this comprehensive web site will fill you with information. See what other mechanical engineers are doing every day, and become a member of this progressive and supportive society. Check them out at http://www.asme.org/.

INDUSTRIAL ENGINEERING

Industrial engineers figure out how to improve everything. They work with people to help them do things better. Industrial engineers save employers money by streamlining systems, often making the workplace better for employees too. They improve productivity and quality while saving time and money.

Industrial engineers work on all type of businesses. They see the big picture and focus on what makes a system perform efficiently, safely, and effectively to produce the highest quality.

Industrial engineers work in many different types of organizations. They may be applying their special skills in hospitals, banks, manufacturing plants, insurance companies, or government agencies. Major employers of industrial engineers include corporations such as Microsoft, Boeing, Disney, Intel, and Nike. And, the list goes on.

As an industrial engineer, you may look for new ways to do things better. You may try to automate agencies which require their customers to wait in long lines. You may find ways to make sure employees always have what they need to complete their job. You may survey locations to find the best place to build a major facility.

The Institute of Industrial Engineers (IIE) has good web site at http://www.iienet.org/. The site is full of great information for students. The Institute recognizes outstanding students, offers several scholarships, and has annual competitions.

AGRICULTURAL ENGINEERING

Agricultural engineers design farms, food processing equipment, livestock buildings, and crop storage. They develop systems for irrigation, waste removal, and drainage. The future of agricultural engineering is very bright. Engineers are constantly seeking new ways to grow plants in non-traditional environments. One engineer may work in a lab studying the effects on corn or wheat grown inside, or grown with less light, less water, or less dirt.

Some agricultural engineers may work on developing pesticides that are non-toxic, and some may work developing stronger and more efficient farm equipment such as tractors. Additionally, instruments to test the safety of food and water supplies may be developed by agricultural engineers. High-tech agricultural engineers may work on computer systems to automate large farms.

Visit the ASAE website at http://asae.org/ for more information.

FEATURE ARTICLE

Oceans of Opportunity

As a boy growing up in Nanjing, China, Jaw-Kai Wang had never heard of an agricultural engineer. But a professor at National Taiwan University changed all that when he made Wang an offer he couldn't refuse. "If you want to save the world, this is where you begin," the professor said. Those words lured Wang into the program at the university where he would later graduate with a bachelor's degree in agricultural engineering. He then relocated to the United States and continued his education at Michigan State University where he earned a master's degree and Ph.D. in agricultural engineering. He is now professor of biosystems engineering at the University of Hawaii. After teaching agricultural machine design for several years, Wang's interests turned from land to water. In the late 1970's, one of his graduate students began a project to study prawns, which are edible crustaceans that resemble shrimp. Wang secured funding to start and maintain an "aquaculture" program at the school. Since then, he has made major breakthroughs in raising shrimp and oysters for mass production and is developing some innovative uses for algae. "We are agricultural engineers," Wang says. "What we do best is to grow things. To produce things from biological systems." By 1989, Wang had developed a way to improve oyster and shrimp production. He designed an aquaculture system for raising shrimp and prawns and soon noticed a water quality problem caused by a buildup of uneaten food and shrimp droppings. He found that he could put algae, which feeds on the wastes, in the water with the shrimp.

When the water is clean, the algae is pumped into a separate tank housing oysters. Because the algae floats, Wang designed a fluidized bed to float the oysters on a column of water. The oysters can then eat the algae. This system is patented and a company in Hawaii is using it. Currently, Wang is working toward getting a patent on an antibiotic made from algae. The drug, which kills infection-causing bacteria such as staphylococcus, is being tested on animals and could someday be used against bacteria that has become resistant to existing drugs. Wang says algae has many other uses, including as a food coloring. "People have never bothered much to look at it," he says. "There is nothing but potential here. It's so interesting." Wang predicts that within the next 10 years, jobs in aquaculture will be plentiful as fish production becomes important as a food source. He believes that an agricultural and biological engineering background allows people entering this field to be versatile in these areas. At 65, Wang says "there's never a dull moment" in his career. "You put the puzzle together piece by piece."

There will always be a need for production from biological systems." And as for saving the world: "There is still the idealistic part," he says. "To do something useful. To make a contribution. That you should give back to society." *Reprinted from Resources Magazine published by the American Society of Agricultural Engineers.*

AERONAUTICAL / AEROSPACE ENGINEERING

Aeronautical/aerospace engineering is the profession that designs and develops technology for commercial aviation, national defense, and space exploration. These engineers may help design and manufacture military aircraft, missiles, and spacecraft. Emphasis is usually placed on the structure of the aircraft, aerodynamics, guidance and control, propulsion and design, manufacturing, or specialization in a certain type of aircraft. Commercial airliners, military aircraft, space shuttles, satellites, rockets, and helicopters are all within the reach of the talented aeronautical engineer. These engineers are also often referred to as astronautical, aviation, and rocket engineers.

Aeronautical/aerospace engineers may work on the hundreds of satellites that orbit the earth or on the commercial and military aircraft that carry millions of passengers. Several other areas include developing materials that can withstand extreme temperatures, investigating biological applications of astronauts in space, and reducing the effects of sonic booms on the environment.

From the Wright Brothers back in 1903 to international space stations, aeronautical/aerospace engineering has enjoyed tremendous growth. Employment is expected to grow faster than the average for most fields. Many jobs are defense related, and budget cuts may eliminate some jobs. However, the need for quieter and more fuel-efficient commercial airplanes as well as the increased demand for spacecraft and helicopters will create many opportunities for aeronautical engineers. It is a very progressive and complex field that will undoubtedly advance much more as mankind attempts to travel beyond the moon to explore the planets.

Registration is required in all fifty states for engineers whose work may affect an individual's life, health, or property. Registration is also required for engineers who offer their services to the public. Hence, professional registration is especially important for aeronautical/aerospace engineers. Learn more aeronautical/aerospace engineering by visiting the Aerospace Engineering Division website of the ASME at http://www.asme.org/.

AUTOMOTIVE ENGINEERING

Automotive engineering is a branch of mechanical engineering where the majority of engineers are employed by major automobile companies. Automobile engineers may research alternative fuel choices, they may study aerodynamics to improve fuel efficiency, or they may improve the suspensions of sports cars or four-wheel-drive vehicles.

Automotive engineers are involved in every aspect of vehicle design. The automotive industry is very competitive, so these engineers can expect to enjoy a future of growth potential in an exciting and challenging environment. Some benefits to automotive engineering is that the engineer is able to experience cutting-edge technology first hand, to be involved in several stages of new car development, and most likely to receive a discount on their own new vehicle!

Visit the Society of Automotive Engineers (SAE) website at http://www.sae.org/ to get more information.

FEATURE ARTICLE

A New Approach To Car Safety: The Moving Seat

Researchers at Illinois Institute of Technology, Chicago, are working on a new approach to automobile safety based on a moving seat that reduces the effect of a collision on the passenger.

Instead of the conventional seat which is bolted rigidly to the automobile chassis, the new seat under investigation features an attachment through a computer-based actuator. At impact the seat moves in the direction specified by the actuator, reducing the effect of the crash on the pasenger.

"The motion allows some of the energy of the crash to be absorbed by the system," explains Nabeel Tarabishy, Ph.D., a visiting professor at the institute and member of ASME International (American Society of Mechanical Engineers).

Dr. Tarabishy and his colleagues have created computer models and simulations showing the dynamics of a human passenger in the moving seat during a collision. Based on the data, the researchers believe that a moving seat can make a 35 mile-per-hour impact feel only like a 23 mile-per-hour jolt, thereby reducing potential head injury.

Dr. Tarabishy says that further research will be required to address ways in which the moving seat may be synchronized with air bags. The researchers also admit that their computer models are simple and very preliminary, meaning sled tests are necessary to determine implementation issues.

Dr. Tarabishy believes that automobile companies may be able to justify the high costs associated with new safety designs because "more and more customers are demanding safer cars." The moving seat can also be built into trucks and airplanes, says Tarabishy.

Dr. Tarabishy's research, involving
such phenomena as energy absorption, dy-
namic systems and control, and computer-
aided design, demonstrates the contribution
engineers make to human safety each and
every day. *Reprinted with the permission of
the American Society of Mechanical Engineers.*

HEATING, VENTILATING, REFRIGERATING, AND AIR-CONDITIONING ENGINEERING

Heating, ventilating, refrigeration, and air-conditioning
(HVRandAC) engineers have dramatically improved our lives.
HVRandAC engineers develop systems to create and maintain safe and
comfortable environments. Airplanes, trains, schools, cars, and com-
puter rooms are only a handful of the environments that depend on
HVRandAC engineers.

An HVRandAC engineer who has an interest in biology can
develop cryosurgery systems. An HVRandAC engineer with an interest
in transportation can develop refrigerator cars for trains and trucks to
enable transportation of chemicals or freezer foods. An HVRandAC
engineer with an interest in energy conservation can design more efficient heating, ventilating, refrigeration, or air-conditioning systems. Visit
the American Society of Heating, Refrigerating and Air-Conditioning
Engineers website at http://www.ashrae.org/.

FEATURE ARTICLE

Refrigeration, Milton Garland: One "Cool" Engineer

What do ice cubes, air conditioning,
computers, hockey, antibiotics, organ trans-
plants, space exploration, and fresh fruit have
in common? To answer that question, look
around you. Almost everywhere you look you
will see the positive impact of refrigeration

technology. One of the giants of the heating, ventilating, air-conditioning and refrigerating industry is refrigeration engineer and inventor Milton W. Garland. For the past 77 years, he has advanced refrigeration technology through his inventions and his public service. In fact, Garland, who will celebrate his 102nd birthday on August 23, is known throughout the industry as "Mr. Refrigeration."

Garland holds 40 patents and is the developer of refrigeration compressors for industrial and commercial use. But, Garland's most recognizable invention was the first "shell" ice maker, which manufactured ice on the outside of four-inch diameter, ten-foot length tubes. His system was more efficient and sanitary than the then-current system of producing ice in galvanized cans. As a result, demand soared for use in chicken processing plants, for cooling milk containers during deliveries, and developing an industrial air conditioning system in a two-mile deep gold mine, which reduced temperatures from 110 degrees to 90 degrees F.

At its Centennial Meeting, which was held in January, 1996, the American Society of Heating, Refrigerating and Air-Conditioning Engineers, Inc. (ASHRAE), honored Garland, a Fellow and Life Member, as an ASHRAE Centennial Honoree: A Pioneer in Technology.

Garland obtained his first experience with refrigeration engineering in the U.S. Navy during World War I. In 1920, he graduated from Worcester Polytechnic Institute in Massachusetts, and joined the Frick Company, in Waynesboro, Pennsylvania. Over the next half century, he served in the positions of field installation trainee, chief engineer, vice president of engineering, and vice president of technical services.

Of his career Garland says, "I wanted to be an engineer ever since I was a little boy. Someway, somehow, I was going to be an engineer." And, now 77 years later, the word "retire" simply isn't in his vocabulary. Since 1967, he has continued to work part time as senior consultant of technical services and patent coordinator at Frick.

Garland plays golf once a week, and he is an avid hockey fan. And why not? He helped engineer the refrigeration system for the Hershey Bears' ice rink in Hershey, Pennsylvania. He and his wife, Alice, have been known to drive 140 miles round trip during the winter to see a home game. *Reprinted courtesy of the American Society of Heating, Refrigerating and Air-Conditioning Engineers, Inc.*

MANUFACTURING ENGINEERING

If the mechanical engineer designs parts, the manufacturing engineer designs the processes that make them. You find manufacturing engineers in Detroit's big-three production facilities overseeing plants of the major computer companies, directing six-person mold and die shops that make advanced prototypes, and working on teams in the football-field-sized structures where Boeing assembles jumbo jets. Wherever there's a production process to be designed and managed, you'll find manufacturing engineers at work.

Manufacturing engineers need in-depth training and aptitude for basic engineering principles, a disciplined approach to work, and creativity. Because the focus is the process, not the individual part, they see things through a wider-angle lens. They bring their particular brand of insight to teams. They work with plant managers, production supervisors, CNC programmers, quality managers, product designers, and R&D staff on issues ranging from evaluating new technology and choosing equipment and suppliers, to leading industry-wide standards development, to reorganizing the plant into a more efficient production system.

Negotiation skills and the ability to sell ideas are essential. Ford Motor Co. puts interpersonal skills on the list of skills manufacturing engineers need, right after basic engineering. Ford's manufacturing engineers must work closely with product designers and communicate with them on the same technical level. The goal is not to make a designer out of the manufacturing engineer, but to get design and manufacturing to work seamlessly together to make the highest quality, lowest cost possible.

During the last two decades, most major U.S. companies have turned their attention to the plant floor, discovering that the way they made their products was a strategic advantage in the growing global marketplace. Manufacturing engineers led the way by championing key concepts including lean production, agile manufacturing, re-engineering, and continuous improvement.

Manufacturing engineers must do more than make and deliver products competitively. They must use their "system thinking" to understand what role manufacturing plays in the overall business and how to customize products to meet the needs and suit the tastes of customers around the world.

The Society of Manufactuing Engineers (SME), certifies manufacturing engineers (CmfgE) and technologists (CMfgT). It reports more than 7,700 people hold CmfgE certification and some 4,450 hold a CMfgT. In most states, professional registration is available in manufacturing engineering through a state-sponsored examination.

To attract young people to the field, SME sponsors activities like an annual student robotics/automation contest with hundreds of entries from middle school through college (two thirteen-year-olds won the 1997 grand prize), a competition for engineering at its WESTEC California-based trade show, and the JETS (Junior Engineering Technical Society) National Engineering Challenge.

SME members encourage manfacturing engineering careers for young people. Chapter 207 (Charleston, SC), for example, sponsors a summer manufacturing boot camp at Trident Technical College where eighth-graders get hands-on experience designing a product using CAD and rapid prototyping, then produce it using CNC equipment and check quality on a coordinate measuring machine. When they're not designing or making parts, boot-camp participants visit local major manufacturing companies like Robert Bosch Corp. and Cummins Engine Co. to amplify the learning experience.

FEATURE ARTICLE

From Cows to Cape Kennedy

Mark Senti grew up in western Wisconsin's dairy country and farmed for eight years after high school, but lush fields and fat cows were not his destiny. He liked learning about technology, so in 1986 he enrolled in Chippewa Valley Technical College, nearby in Eau Claire. There he joined the SME student chapter, received an associate's degree in manufacturing engineering technology, and began to collect awards. The American Technical Education Association named him the nation's outstanding technical student.

When Senti joined Cray Research in Chippewa Falls as a manufacturing engineer, he revolutionized the wiring and testing of computer chassis and its interconnect-packaging technology, using a flexible manufacturing system approach. In 1990 Cray honored him for research leadership and innovation. In 1992 he won SME's Outstanding Young Manufacturing Engineer award. It turned out to be a good predictor.

Today he is CEO of GMSA Systems, which provides industry with robotic and automation systems. At the same time he serves as vice president and director of Advanced Magnet Lab, which designs and manufactures superconducting magnets. AML recently built a world-record 4.3Tesla superconducting accelerator magnet. The two companies are in Palm Bay, Florida where the Senti family likes to go to Cape Kennedy to watch the Space Shuttle launches. Senti, who is on the board of advisors of Florida Institute of Technology, has a passion for technical education and plans to get CmfgE accreditation soon. *Reprinted courtesy of the Society of Manufacturing Engineers.*

SME maintains an Internet website at http://www.sme.org/ that offers extensive information on this discipline, as well as provides electronic links among hundreds of member chapters, affiliated technical associations in robots, plastics, electronics, machine vision, and others. See Appendix for more contact information.

ROBOTIC ENGINEERING

Robotic engineering is an exciting field that is quickly developing a wide range of applications. Because of the technological leaps that the computer industry is making, many new opportunities will emerge for robotic engineers. Robotic engineers design robots, maintain robots, and research new applications for robots. Robots have enormous potential for society. Equipped with the proper sensors, robots can inspect the quality of meat, measure the pollution emissions of manufacturing plants, assist surgery, detect corrosion in sewer pipes, investigate the depths of a volcano, or assess the speed of a tornado. Robots can improve our standard of living and give us more information about how our planet or even the solar system is made. Such advances can open new doors for space exploration or underwater societies.

Robots have been used primarily in the manufacturing industry, and this industry is still the primary employer of robotics engineers. Automobiles are often built with the aid of a programmable machine that incorporates great precision, speed, and power. Robotics is also expanding to mining, agriculture, and other jobs that are hazardous or undesirable to people. Robotic engineers work very closely with computer programmers, electrical engineers, mechanical and manufacturing engineers, and production managers.

Robotic engineers decide how the controls of a robot will work. For example, a mechanical engineer who is working on robots will design a sensor to detect light, food, tilting, etc., whereas the robotics engineer will design how the sensor will be controlled and incorporated into the robot.

Robot soccer is an excellent example of the complexity involved in creating artificial intelligence. University of Southern California (USC) competed in the first Robot World Cup Initiative (RoboCup) that was held in Japan in 1997. USC had five "soccer-bots" that could spin and twirl on individual spherical truck wheels. The USC "soccer-bots" were created from modified radio-controlled toy trucks. Each robot received a Pentium-powered brain and a digital "eye." The Pentium laptop was mounted onto each player's back and connected to the "eye." Wei-Min Shen, the computer science professor heading the project, said "the complexity of such a task is extraordinary. Just getting the robot to distinguish between a soccer ball and a human leg requires months of programming. Sometimes their eyes detect the red hue in flesh and mistake it for the orange in a soccer ball."

Imagine a robot sensing the location of the orange soccer ball, chasing the ball, outmaneuvering other players, to eventually score a goal. Nearly 100 teams are signed up to compete in the 1998 RoboCup that will be held in Paris, France.

More information about robotic engineering can be found at the Robotics International of the Society of Manufacturing Engineers (RI/SME) website at http://www.sme.org and at the IEEE Robotics and Automation Society website located at http://www.ieee.org/society/ra.html.

Chapter 9

Nuclear Engineering

According to the 1996-97 edition of the
Occupational Outlook Handbook,
the average starting salary for a nuclear engineer
in 1994 was $33,600

Nuclear engineers split atoms to produce power. Many people associate nuclear power with nuclear weapons and radiation spills. Nuclear engineering goes far beyond these traditional negative associations to fall into three major areas of benefit to mankind: nuclear medicine, agricultural uses and pest control, and nuclear energy. Nuclear engineers are in search of efficient and beneficial ways to use the power generated from splitting an atom, and they research ways to use nuclear energy and radiation.

Nuclear medicine engineers may develop new ways to fight cancer with radiation therapies, or they may design equipment that helps diagnose and treat diseases such as imaging devices that use radioactive materials to provide the degree of function present in an organ. X-rays are often used to see pictures of the inside of the body, and CT and MRI machines produce 3-D images of anatomy. However, nuclear medicine can tell the physician if there is a restriction of blood flow to the brain or if a patient's heart has been damaged in a heart attack. Nuclear medicine allows the physician to determine if all parts of a specific organ are functioning properly. This technology significantly reduces hospital admissions and patient costs by often eliminating the need for surgery and hospital stays. Radiation is also used to sterilize medical supplies and develop new drugs.

The United Nations Food and Agriculture Organization reports that pests and bacteria contaminate almost twenty-five percent of the world's food supply every year. Nuclear engineers directly ease the burden of world hunger by developing new ways to preserve food such as irradiation (a process which eliminates disease-causing microorganisms such as salmonella) or even using radiation to produce food (irradiation of seeds can stimulate earlier and more abundant crops.)

Nuclear energy is the largest energy source in the world and the final area of emphasis in nuclear engineering. The fuel is inert, can be recycled many times, and may provide our nation with an unlimited supply of energy.

Nuclear engineering is a challenging and rewarding career. In the United States, nuclear reactors provide about 3.7 million jobs and twenty percent of our electricity needs. Nuclear power plants can recharge the electric cars of the future. Nuclear energy can power pumps that carry water from the ocean to desalination plants and then out to wherever it is needed. Nuclear power can generate electricity. Nuclear engineers may run particle accelerators or test nuclear equipment.

The U.S. Navy operates half the nuclear power reactors in the United States aboard surface ships and submarines. Nuclear power allows ships to travel at high speeds for years without refueling. For example, the first nuclear-powered submarine, USS Nautilus, operated on nuclear power for more than two years and covered 62,562 miles before refueling. In contrast, a diesel-powered ship would use two million gallons of fuel to cover the same number of miles.

The potential of nuclear power is essentially boundless. Nuclear medicine procedures are painless and among the safest diagnostic imaging tests available. Finding ways to harness nuclear power may save many of the earth's resources. According to the American Nuclear Society, nuclear power creates no global warming or harmful air pollution.

The American Nuclear Society (ANS) has a great web site that has information on student branches, scholarships, internships, and exchanges at http://www.ans.org/. The site also has some good articles about nuclear power and its effects on society.

Bibliography/ Recommended Reading

Basta, Nicholas, *Opportunities in Engineering Careers*, VGM Career Horizons: 1990.

Belcher, M. Clay, "What is Architectural Engineering?" University of Kansas: 1993.

Bolles, Richard Nelson, *What Color is your Parachute?: A Practical Manual for Job Hunters and Career Changers*, Ten Speed Press: 1993.

"Careers in Science and Engineering: A Student Guide to Grad School and Beyond," National Academy Press:1996.

Crowl, Barbara and Karen Franklin, "A New and Improved 'Tech Act,' " A.T. Quarterly: 1994.

Ercolano, Vincent, "Mother-Daughter Academy," ASEE PRISM. Feb. 1998.

Etzkowitz, Henry, Carol Kemelgor, and Michael Neuschatz, "Barriers to Women in Academic Science and Engineering," John Hopkins University Press: 1994.

Ferrell, Tom, "Workplace 2000: Engineering," Peterson's Job Opportunities for Engineering and Computer Science Majors 1998.

Gabelman, Irving , "The New Engineer's Guide to Career Growth and Professional Awareness," IEEE Press: 1996.

"The Green Report: Engineering Education for a Changing World," American Society for Engineering Education:1998.

Landis, Raymond, "Enhancing Student Success: A Five Step Process for Getting Students to "Study Smart," American Society for Engineering Education:1998.

Landis, Raymond, "Enhancing Engineering Student Success: A Pedagogy for Changing Behaviors,":1997.

Landis, Raymond B., *Studying Engineering: A Roadmap to a Rewarding Career,* Discovery Press: 1995.

LeBold, William K. and Dona J. LeBold, "Women Engineers: A Historical Perspective," American Society for Engineering Education:1998.

Love, Sydney F., *Planning and Creating Successful Engineered Designs: Managing the Design Process*, Advanced Professional Development Incorporated: 1986.

Morgan, Robert P., Proctor P. Reid, and Wm, A. Wulf, "The Changing Nature of Engineering," ASEE PRISM. May-June 1998.

Nekuda, Jennifer, *Structural Engineering*, University of Kansas: 1997.

Paula, Greg, "Cobots for the Assembly Line," Mechanical Engineering: 1997.

Peterson, George D. "Engineering Criteria 2000: A Bold New Change Agent," American Society for Engineering Education:1998.

"Planning a Career in Biomedical Engineering," Biomedical Engineering Society: 1996.

Sherwood, Kaitlin, "Women in the Engineering Industry," Society of Women Engineers at UIUC lecture: 1994.

"Simple Machines", Society of Women Engineers Career Guidance Module: 1996.

"Student Science Training Programs for Precollege Students," Science Service, Inc.: 1994.

Tieger, Paul and Barbara Barron-Tieger, *Do What You Are: Discover the Perfect Career for You through the Secrets of Personality Type*, Little, Brown and Company:1995.

"Today's News and Views for Tomorrow's Engineers," *The ASME Mechanical Advantage:* 1997.

Vanderheiden, Gregg, "Thirty Something (Million): Should they be Exceptions?" Trace Research and Development Center, Waisman Center and Department of Industrial Engineering, University of Wisconsin-Madison:1996.

"Women, Minorities, and Persons with Disabilities in Science and Engineering: 1996," The National Science Foundation: 1996.

Yantzi, Lindsay, *The Construction Industry's Orthopedic Specialist*, University of Kansas: 1997.

Learning More

Engineering Camps

The following camp directory lists some of the residential camps for high school students in science, mathematics, and engineering throughout the United States that are and were previously offered. The directory lists camps that have been hosted by Universities and research centers in the past. Please note that all camps may not be offered every year and that new camps and programs are currently being added. Old or unsuccessful programs are always being eliminated or modified. A substantial number of programs specifically target minorities, women, and other groups traditionally underrepresented in the sciences. The programs offered change frequently, and this database is not comprehensive. This Appendix is only meant to be a guide to aid your search for engineering education preparaton tools. Many of the programs offer scholarships and may have application deadlines as early as January. If you are interested in a program, please call or write the organization listed for an applicaton and the most current information avalable.

ALABAMA

Alabama A&M University
Summer Minority High School Student Science Training Program
Features courses in math, general science, English, and computer science, as well as instruction in test preparation skills and career awareness.
CONTACT: Department of Math, Alabama A&M University, P.O. Box 326, Normal, AL 35762 (205/851-5300).

Auburn University (call for additional programs)
Future Life Science Scholars Program
Offers faculty-guided research experiences and integrated life science/chemistry courses. Designed for students interested in pursuing careers in teahing and research in biomedical sciences.
CONTACT: Dean's Office, Extension Cottage, Auburn University, Auburn, AL 36849 (334/844-4269).

Marine Environmental Sciences Consortium/Dauphin Island Sea Lab
Discovery Hall Program
CONTACT: Registrar's Office, Discovery Hall Program, P.O. Box 369-370, Dauphin Island, AL 36528 (205/861-7540).

Tuskegee University (call for additional programs)
Freshmen Accelerated Start-Up and Training for Retention in Engineering Curricula (FASTREC)
Highlights courses in precalculus, engineering graphics, and computer programming.
Minority Introduction to Engineering (MITE)
Introduces all aspects of engineering through course work and lectures.
CONTACT: Associate Dean, School of Engineering, Architecture, and Physical Sciences, Tuskegee University, Tuskegee, AL 36088 (334/727-8356).

ALASKA
Foundation for Glacier and Environmental Research in Cooperation with the University of Idaho and the University of Alaska Southeast
Summer Glaciological and Arctic Studies Expeditionary Institute for Young Scholars
Spotlights field experience and research involvement in environmental science, field geology, glaciology, geophysics, arctic ecology, meteorology, survey and mapping, computer applications to field data, and research analysis. Teaches survival skills and practical expeditionary training in a spectacular and physically demanding mountain and arctic environment.
CONTACT: Foundaion for Glacier and Environmental Research, 514 East First St., Moscow, ID 83843 (208/882-1237), (208/885-6382)or (208/885-6192).

ARIZONA
Arizona State University
Center for Academic Precocity (CAP)
Features many research opportunities and courses in math, science, computers, and humanities.
CONTACT: Center for Academic Precocity, College of Education, ASU, Box 872711, Tempe, AZ 85287-2711 (602/965-4757).

University of Arizona
Horizons Unlimited; The Science Program
Features courses in genetic engineering, environmental sciences, solar energy, landscape architecture, plant diseases, human behavior and development, computer applications in natural sciences, entomology, nutritional sciences, and animal science.
CONTACT: Program Coordinator, Office of Academic Programs, Forbes Bldg., Rm. 211, Tucson, AZ 85721 (520/621-2211) or (520/621-1374).

White Mountain Archaeological Center
Basic Field Archaeology and Laboratory Curation
Emphasizes classical training in archaeological field research. Includes survey, mapping, excavation, artifact handling, cleaning and classification, com-

puter cataloging and recreation, artifact reconstruction, site stabilization and reconstruction.
CONTACT: White Mountain Archaeological Center, HC 30, Box 30, St. John's, AZ 85936 (520/333-5857).

ARKANSAS
Hendrix College
Arkansas Governor's School
Offers a comprehensive liberal arts curriculum with emphasis on theory, paradigms, critical analysis, and apistenology.
CONTACT: Arkansas high school G/T coordinator/counselors.

CALIFORNIA
California State University, Sacramento
Chicano-Latino Youth Math, Engineering, and Science Symposium (CLYMESS)
Features hands-on activities in math and science designed to expose students to contributions by American Indian and Latino role models. Students design rockets and go on industry tours which promote interaction with professional engineers. Includes components on college applications and peer counselor interaction.
CONTACT: CLYMESS, School of Engineering and Computer Science, California State University, Sacramento, CA 95819-6023 (916/278-7504).

Occidental College
Oceanology at Occidental College
Introduces marine biology, including the taxonomy of plankton, algae, invertebrates, fish, and mammals. Emphasizes ecology, touching on marine chemistry and geology, and pollution. Activities are centered around the use of an 85-foot research essel, the Vantuna.
CONTACT: Department of Biology, Occidental College, Los Angeles, CA 90041 (213/259-2890).

Santa Catalina School
Summer Marine Biology Program
Spotlights marine biology including lectures, lab and field work, a research paper, and a final exam. One year high school credit.
CONTACT: Summer Programs, Santa Catalina School, 1500 Mark Thomas Drive, Monterey, CA 93940 (408/655-9386).

The Thacher School
Summer Science Program
Features non-credit instruction in physics, astronomy, math, and computer science. Team projects supplement lectures and focus on professional-grade telescopes to determine the elements of the orbit of a minor planet.

CONTACT: Administrative Director, The Thacher School, Ojai, CA 93023 (805/ 646-4377).

University of California, Davis
Engineering Summer Residency Program (ESRP)
Explores engineering education through hands-on lab work, lectures, design competitions, writing exercises, workshops on applying to college and for financial aid, and field trips.
CONTACT: Special Programs Director, University of California - Davis, 1050E Engineering II, Dean's Office, Davis, CA 95616 (530/752-3316).

University of California, San Diego
Precollege Summer Scholars Program
Held in collaboration with the Scripps Institution of Oceanography. Highlights marine biology and American politics through lectures, discussions, projects, and field trips. Students sample college life by living on campus and participating in sports events and social activities.
CONTACT: UCSD Precollege Summer Scholars Program, University of California, 0179, La Jolla, CA 92093-0179 (619/534-7074).

University of California, Santa Barbara (call for additional programs)
High School Juniors Program
Offers qualified students up to 12 units of university credit in disciplines chosen from more than 90 lower division courses. The residence hall offers students a special tutorial center, guidance and counseling office and EOP/ SAA advisors, along with many planned and impromptu social events. Offers SAT workshops. Intramural sports culminate in Tournament Day.
Young Scholars Summer Program
Offers a unique curriculum for gifted and talented students in art, biology, literature, and math. Taught in seminar, studio, and tutorial formats, courses instill desire for advanced and independent work. Students may also enroll in regular Summer Sessions classes complementary to the YSSP curriculum. SAT workshops are offered. Professional staff teaches students about residence hall life and relaxation.
CONTACT: Coordinator, UCSB Summer Sessions, Santa Barbara, CA 93106-2010 (805/893-2047 x2010).

COLORADO
American Indian Science and Engineering Society (AISES) (call for additional programs)
Precollege Enrichment Programs
Promotes academic and cultural enrichment through interaction with American Indian role models in science, engineering, and math-related professions. Covers mathematics, health sciences, physical sciences, life sciences, computer sciences, engineering, and environmental sciences.

CONTACT: Director of Precollege Programs, AISES, 5661 Airport Blvd., Boulder, CO 80301-2339 (303/939-0023). (Programs held in WI, NM, IA. MT, CA, NY, and CO.) Several other programs also offered; call or visit website for updated information.

Colorado State University
Science Motivation Program
Matches students' interests with research areas such as physiology, microbiology, pathology, clinical science, chemistry, biochemistry, neurobiology, radiation biology, and environmental health.
CONTACT: Summer Programs Office, Colorado State University, Fort Collins, CO 80523 (970/491-1590).

Crow Canyon Archaeological Center
High School Field School
Students perform field and lab research as actual partners with Crow Canyon's research team of archaeologists.
CONTACT: Registrar, Crow Canyon Arch'l Ctr., 23390 County Rd. K, Cortez, CO 81321 (970/565-8975, ext. 130).

University of Colorado at Boulder
Young Scholars Summer Session
Focuses on one college-level course for which students receive 3 college credits, and they are taught by faculty with reputations for excellent teaching. Numerous recreational and cultural activities.
CONTACT: Young Scholars Summer Session, UC at Boulder, Campus Box 73, Boulder, CO 80309-0073 (303/492-5421).

University of Denver (call for additional programs)
The Making of an Engineer
Surveys engineering disciplines including electrical, computer, and mechanical engineering. Includes academy periods, individual projects in robotics, superconductors, bioengineering, and career counseling. Uses digital systems for engineering design.
CONTACT: Bureau of Educational Services, University of Denver, Wesley Hall 203, Denver, CO 80208 (303/871-2663).
Rocky Mountain Talent Search Summer Institute
Features intensive courses in math, psychology, science, communications, international studies, and theater.
CONTACT: Rocky Mountain Talent Search, University of Denver, Wesley Hall, Room 203, 2135 E. Wesley Ave., Denver, CO 80208 (303/871-2983).

University of Northern Colorado
Frontiers of Science Institute

Intensive science program covering the disciplines of biological, physical, computer, energy/geology, and environmental sciences. Includes classroom and field work as well as completion of individual science project.
CONTACT: University of Northern Colorado, Ross Hall 215, Greeley, CO 80639 (970/351-2976 or 970/351-1890).

CONNECTICUT
Post College (Waterbury)
National Computer Camps
Features courses in computer science and programming.
CONTACT: Director, Nat'l Computer Camps, P.O. Box 585, Orange, CT 06477 (203/795-9667 or 408/554-5763). (Programs also offered in Atlanta, GA; Santa Clara, CA; and Cleveland, OH).

University of Connecticut (call for additional programs)
Summer Bridge Program
Introduces engineering curriculum, including college-level chemistry, physics, computer science, and math.
CONTACT: Director, Engineering Diversity Program, School of Engineering, Office of the Dean, U-237M, 191 Auditorium Rd., Storrs, CT 06269-3237 (860/486-5536 or 860/486-2000).
Upward Bound/HSCP
Students take four main academic courses; two English classes (composition and literature), science, and math. Assigns students to a special project designed to promote a collaborative learning environment to foster group communication skills while exploring topics of interest. Past special projects have focused on law, business, physics, biology, and geography.
CONTACT: University of Connecticut, Upward Bound/HSCP, 341 Mansfield Road, Storrs, CT 06269-1170 (860/486-4040 or 860/486-2000).

Yale University
Yale Summer Programs
Offers courses in anthropology, astronomy, biology, chemistry, computer science, calculus, psychology, sociology, and statistics for highly qualified high school seniors or grads.
CONTACT: Director and Dean, Yale College, Yale Summer Programs, 246 Church St., Ste. 101, New Haven, CT 06510-1722 (203/432-2430).

DELAWARE
Delaware State University (call for additional programs)
Forum to Advance Minorities in Engineering (FAME)
A precollege engineering program which prepares and motivates minority students to enter and complete a baccalaureate of science program in engineering.
Intensive Summer Science Program (ISSP)

Designed to help minority students make their mathematics functional, to provide instruction in biology, chemistry. and physics, and physics from an interdisciplinary approach to enhance communication skills and to demonstrate the role of the computer in preparing for careers in an information-based society.
CONTACT: Delaware State University, 1200 N. Dupont Hwy., Dover, DE 19901 (302/739-4924).

University of Delaware
FAME/UD
Features research and course work in algebra, precalculus, calculus, chemistry, physics, English, computer orientation, and engineering design. Includes college advising and professional development workshops.
CONTACT: Assistant Dean and Director, 135 du Pont Hall, College of Engineering, University of Delaware, Newark, DE 19716 (302/831-6315).
John Henry Taylor Scholars
Features courses in math, science, English, and study skills, as well as individual and group tutorial sessions.
CONTACT: Academic Services Center, University of Delaware, 5 W. Main Street, George Evans House, Newark, DE 19716 (302/831-2805).
Summer College
Features college credit biology, chemistry, and math courses for academically advanced students--a taste of college life and academics.
CONTACT: Summer College Honors Program, University of Delaware, Newark, DE 19716 (302/831-8741).

DISTRICT OF COLUMBIA
Catholic University of America
Engineering 2000
Features a tour of engineering which includes six plenary sessions by speakers of national stature, plus participation in two research projects in biomedical, civil, electrical, and mechanical engineering, and computer science.
CONTACT: Assistant to the Dean, Catholic University of America, Washington, DC 20064 (202/319-5160).

Georgetown University
Georgetown Amateur Scientist Program (GASP)
Offers hands-on activities in biology, chemistry, physics, and pre-engineering. Features educational field trips, personal counseling, and career guidance.
CONTACT: Georgetown University, Center for Minority Student Affairs, P.O. Box 2266, Washington, DC 20057-1003 (202/687-0100).

Quality Education for Minorities (QEM) Network
NASA SHARP PLUS

Establishes individual working relationships between minority students and active science and engineering researchers in aerospace-related fields. Students live on campus, carry out research assignments with mentors, prepare written reports, and make oral presentations.
CONTACT: Assistant Director, Communications, QEM Network, 1818 N St., NW, Ste. 350, Washington, DC 20036 (202/659-1818).

FLORIDA
Embry-Riddle Aeronautical University (call for additional programs)
ACES Academy
Highlights research and courses in aviation fundamentals and career choices available in the fields of aerospace and aviation. Topics include flight theory, aircraft design, aviation maintenance, meteorology, aviation history, aviation management with computer applications, and flight simulation.
CONTACT: Aeronautical Science Department, Embry-Riddle Aeronautical University, TRC/ASSL, Daytona Beach, FL 32114 (904/226-6499).
Sun Flight
Features a flight training program including ground instruction, visits to aviation sites, and aviation career orientation classes in Daytona Beach, FL.
CONTACT: Embry-Riddle Aeronautical University, 600 S. Clyde Morris Blvd., Daytona Beach, FL 32114 (904/226-7648).

Florida Agricultural and Mechanical University (call for additional programs)
Biological Sciences Enhancement
Increases knowledge in the biological sciences and enhances learning and career selection. Features course work, seminars, field trips, and workshops on test-taking and study skills.
Molecular Biology Institute
Increases students awareness of and appreciation for opportunities in biotechnology. Features course work, special projects, seminars, and field trips, as well as test-taking and study skills workshops.
CONTACT: Director, FAMU/BIONR Center, Department of Biology, Florida A&M University, Tallahassee, FL 32307 (850/561-2467)

Florida Atlantic University
The Technology Connection
Features hands-on experiences in six engineering labs to create a zest for learning and a curiosity about engineering, science, and technology. Includes field trips to local industry sites and evening cultural activities.
CONTACT: Florida Atlantic University, Precollegiate Programs/MT-2, Boca Raton, FL 33431 (561/297-2680).

University of Florida Center for Precollegiate Education and Training
Student Science Training Program

An intensive, multidisciplinary research program in which participants live on campus. Features lab research with individually assigned lab work with research mentors, a science lecture series, ethics forums, communications workshops, college-level statistics or computer classes, peer study groups, leadership and conflict resolution training, and various unique educational and recreational field trips around Florida.
CONTACT: Center of Precollegiate Education and Training, P.O. Box 112010, Gainesville, FL 32611-2010 (352/392-2310).

University of Miami
Summer Scholars Program in Marine and Atmospheric Science
Students examine the physical structure of the oceans, the chemistry of seawater, and the structure of marine and estuarine ecosystems. Features experiments on research vessels, snorkeling on coral reefs, and studies of the effects of humans on marine life.
CONTACT: Summer Scholar Programs, University of Miami, P.O. Box 248005, Coral Gables, FL 33124-1610 (305/284-2727; toll free: 800/STUDY-UM). Future programs may include broadcasting and journalism, filmmaking, law, and medicine. Call for availability.

GEORGIA
Georgia Institute of Technology (call for additional programs)
Minority Introduction to Engineering (MITE)
Introduces engineering and science through course work and tours.
Precollege Engineering Program (PREP)
Introduces engineering and science through course work and tours.
CONTACT: Office of Minority and Special Programs, College of Engineering, Georgia Institute of Technology, Atlanta, GA 30332-0361 (404/894-3354).

Wesleyan College
SPECTACLES
Encourages girls to pursue math and science. Includes a portion of time at the U.S. Department of Energy's Oak Ridge National Laboratory.
CONTACT: Wesleyan College, 4760 Forsyth Road, Macon, GA 31297 (912/ 477-1110 x359).

HAWAII
University of Hawaii at Hilo
Hawaii-SSTP
Features courses and research in calculus and physics.
CONTACT: Hawaii-SSTP, University of Hawaii, Hilo, HI 96720-4091 (808/ 974-7311).

IDAHO
University of Idaho (call for additional programs)

Idaho Science Camp
Features course work, lectures, and hands-on studies in math, engineering, physical sciences, and environmental sciences.
Minority Engineering Technical Society (JETS) Summer Workshop
Areas of study include computer-aided design, engineering, and human factors.
CONTACT: College of Engineering, University of Idaho, Moscow, ID 83844-1011 (208/885-6438).

ILLINOIS
Center for American Archaeology
Education Program
Trains students in excavation and analysis by working with professional archaeologists and individual mentors to design and conduct individual research projects in bioanthropology, geology, and botany.
CONTACT: Director of Education, Center for American Archaeology, Kampsville Archaeology Center, P.O. Box 366, Kampsville, IL 62053 (618/653-4316).

Northwestern University (call for additional programs)
National High School Instiute, Engineering and Science Division
Offers research and courses in mathematics, chemistry, physics, biology, engineering, biomedical engineering, and computer science.
CONTACT: Northwestern University, Nat'l High School Institute, 2299 N. Campus Dr., Evanston, IL 60208 (847/491-3026; 800/662-6474).
Academy Program
Intensive, fast-paced courses in biology, chemistry, human evolution, and material sciences to develop the academic potential of young students.
Center for Talent Development (CTD) Apogee Program
Students take one three-week course in mathematics, computers, drama, literature, philosophy, foreign language, or hands-on science.
Center for Talent Development (CTD) Spectrum Program
Students take one intensive. fast-paced course in precalculus, mathematics, statistics and probability, biology, chemistry, human evolution, topics in physics, Latin, literary analysis, nonfiction writing, creative writing, computer science, American economic behavior, introduction to philosophy, and others. Classes meet five hours per day, five days per week. Daily study hall is required.
Equinox Program
Offers an invigorating mix of challenging course work, social activities, and cultural enrichment. Encourages self-governance in the classroom and dormitory. Offers courses in AP English Literature, AP Language and Composition, AP European History, Mathematics, and Science.
Solstice Program

Academically talented students take one of three courses in mathematics, science, and the humanities. Classes are supplemented by interdisciplinary seminars and cultural activities. Fosters close relationships among students and staff who live on campus with students. Students are given the autonomy and expected to accept the responsibilities of college-aged adults.
CONTACT: Center for Talent Development, Northwestern University, 617 Dartmouth Place, Evanston, IL 60208 (847/491-3782).

Parks College of St. Louis University
Careers in Aerospace Summer Camp
Investigates all aspects of the aerospace industry.
CONTACT: Summer Aerospace Camp, Parks College of St. Louis University, Cahokia, IL 62206 (618/337-7575, ext. 364).

University of Illinois, Urbana-Champaign (call for additional programs)
Futures in Science and Technology
Focuses on applied science projects, courses, and seminars and counseling sessions on career guidance.
Illinois Aerospace Institute
Explores aeronautical and astronautical applications, including theory of flight, aerodynamics, design, systems, and models.
Jr. Engineering Technical Society (JETS) Summer Program in Engineering
Introduces engineering curricula, emphasizing lab and team problem-solving. Includes college planning, study habits, computer-aided design, and roundtables with undergrad/graduate students and professional engineers.
Minority Introduction to Engineering (MITE)
Introduces engineering curricula, emphasizing lab and team problem-solving. Schedule includes planning for college, study habits, computer-aided design and roundtables with undergrad/graduate students and professional engineers.
CONTACT: College of Engineering, University of Illinois, 3-137 ESB, 1101 West Springfield Ave., Urbana, IL 61801 (800/943-5410).

INDIANA
Ball State University
Lasers and Holography: Intro. to Analog and Digital Electronics
Lab intensive and hands-on experience.
CONTACT: Ball State University, Department of Physics and Astronomy, Muncie, IN 47306 (765/285-8860).

DePauw University
OPTIONS
Features core programs in computers (emphasizes applications in science), chemistry (focuses on organic compounds), biology (centers on human biol-

ogy and genetics), and physics (deals with size of universe). Lab work includes the McKim Observatory.
CONTACT: DePauw University, 500 E. Seminary St., Greencastle, IN 46135 (765/658-4359).

Indiana State University
Summer Honors Program
An intensive, intellectually challenging collegiate experience for two college credits in one of over twenty academic areas including aerospace technology, archaeology, business, computer-aided design and manufacturing, math and computer technology, physics, English, French, German, chemistry, nursing.
CONTACT: Indiana State University, Summer Honors Program, Terre Haute, IN 47809 (812/237-2335; 800/234-1639, x 2335).

Indiana University, Bloomington
Exploration of Careers in Science
Covers various science disciplines through a series of lectures, field trips, and lab experiments. Includes research projects under the auspices of university scientists.
CONTACT: Indiana University, Exploration of Careers in Science, Kirkwood Hall #207, Indiana University, Bloomington, IN 47405 (812/855-5397).

Purdue University (call for additional programs)
MITE, PREFACE
Both programs feature engineering programs.
CONTACT: Director, Minority Engineering Program, ENAD Rm. 214, Purdue University, West Lafayette, IN 47907 (765/494-3974).
COMET, STAR, PULSAR, and NOVA
Features challenging course work in science, mathematics, and social sciences. Courses have included chemistry, physics, biology and genetics, comparative anatomy, and scientific instrumentation, among others.
CONTACT: Director of Student Programs, Purdue University, Gifted Education Resource Institute, 1446 LAEB, Room 5114, West Lafayette, IN 47907-1446 (765/494-7243).

Rose-Hulman Institute of Technology
Operation Catapult
Features engineering-related projects, lectures, and computer instruction.
CONTACT: Rose-Hulman Institute of Technology, 55W Wabash Ave., Terre Haute, IN 47903 (812/877-8292).

Tri-State University
Exploring Engineering and Science
Features a variety of courses in engineering.

CONTACT: Secretary to the Dean of Engineering, Tri-State University, Angola, IN 46703 (219/665-4188; 800/347-4878).

IOWA
Iowa State University (call for additional programs)
Challenges for Youth - Talented and Gifted (CY-TAG)
Immerses students in 99 hours of class and lab experiences in physical and biological sciences. Individual program offers precalculus equivalent to high school math course.
EXPLORATIONS!
Introduces an advanced subject in science-related areas of astronomy, physics, robotics, and ecology to stimulate further self-explorations in areas of interest.
Iowa Scholars Academy
Introduces gifted students to rigorous and challenging university life in a supervised, supportive environment. Offers up to 10 university credits for appropriate ISU summer courses. Includes honors seminars, cultural and social events, and recreational activities.
CONTACT: Iowa State University, W172 Lagomarcino Hall, Ames, IA 50011-3180 (515/294-1772).
Program for Women in Science and Engineering Summer Research Internships
Interns earn a stipend while working in an ISU science/engineering research lab and attending weekly seminars. Students present poster at session's end. Requires students to live on campus unless living at home.
CONTACT: Program for Women in Science and Engineering, Iowa State University, 210 Lab of Mechanics, Ames, IA 50011-2130 (515/294-9964).

University of Iowa (call for additional programs)
Secondary Student Training Program; Research Participation Program
Features a defined research project under a scientist's guidance. Topics include medicine, dentistry, pharmacy, engineering, computer science, biological science, physical science, or social science.
CONTACT: Iowa SSTP, Office of the Provost, 111 Jessup Hall, The University of Iowa, Iowa City, IA 52242 (319/335-0040; 800/336-6463).

KANSAS
Kansas State University
Mid-America Consortium for Engineering and Science Achievement (MACESA) Summer Institute
Features sessions in math, science, and engineering. Stresses hands-on lab work, field trips, and speakers.
CONTACT: Director, Minority Engineering Program, 144 Durland Hall, KS University, Manhattan, KS 66506 (913/532-7127).

Pittsburg State University
Superior and Unique Methods of Motivation for the Intellectually Talented (SUMMIT)
Focuses on hands-on experience in chemistry, creative writing, art, math, science fiction, technology, business, and field biology. Provides academic and social activities to encourage self-directed learning and to improve self-concept.
CONTACT: SUMMIT Coordinator, Div. of Continuing Studies, Pittsurg State University, Pittsburg, KS 66762 (316/235-4179).

KENTUCKY

Berea College
Science Focus
Features courses in mathematical problem-solving, and reading and study skills. Includes science-related field trips designed to spark interestin the science fields.
CONTACT: Science Focus, CPO 1924, Berea College, Berea, KY 40404 (606/986-9341 x5391).

Georgetown College
Precollege Academic Experience in Math and Science
Features academically challenging classroom and hands-on lab experiences in biology, chemistry, computer science, and math. Integrated to show applications in all areas.
CONTACT: Biology, Georgetown College, 400 E. College St., Georgetown, KY 40324 (502/863-8088).

Transylvania University (call for additional programs)
Academic Camp with Computer Emphasis
Mixes academics and fun recreational activities. Courses cover one academic area per day including computer science, math, physics, biology, chemistry, psychology, business, and art.
Science and Technology Camp
Features course work, field trips, and recreational activities which make for an exciting summer camp. Stresses a different area each day in math, physics, biology, computer science, and chemistry.
CONTACT: Natural Sciences and Math, Transylvania University, 300 N. Broadway, Lexington, KY 40508 (606/233-8155).

University of Kentucky
Kentucky-Appalachian Science Enrichment Program (KASEP)
Highlights courses and hands-on experiences in science and math. Includes career-oriented field trips.

CONTACT: University of Kentucky, 915 S. Limestone St., Lexington, KY 40536-9824 (606/257-8431).

LOUISIANA
Louisiana State University (call for additional programs)
Mini-Courses and Residence Program
Offers mini-courses in science, art, and humanities. Includes genetic engineering, veterinary medicine, astronomy, ethics, marine biology, biology, chemistry, and math (pre-algebra to calculus).
CONTACT: LSU, 177 Pleasant Hall, Baton Rouge, LA 70803-1520 (800/388-3883 or 504/388-6621).

Northwestern State University
ADVANCE Program for Young Scholars
Features intensive, fast-paced courses in the humanities, the social sciences, mathematics, and computer science; generally, students finish the equivalent to one year of high school work or a semester of college-level work. Offered in conjunction with Duke University's Talent Identification Program.
CONTACT: Programs for the Gifted and Talented, 124 Russell Hall, Northwestern State University, Natchitoches, LA 71497 (318/357-4500).

Southern University
U.S. Department of Energy Environmental Management Precollege Analytical Chemistry (EMPAC) Program
College-level analytical chemistry for university credit. Includes lecture and lab.
CONTACT: Department of Chemistry, Southern University, Baton Rouge, LA 70813 (504/771-3721).

University of Southwestern Louisiana (call for additional programs)
Advanced Early Admission Program
Features courses in math, statistics, computer science, biology, microbiology, chemistry, geology, physics, and engineering.
Summer Early Admission Program
Features courses in math, statistics, computer science, biology, microbiology, chemistry, geology, physics, and engineering.
CONTACT: University of Southwestern Louisiana, High School Relations, P.O. Box 44548, Lafayette, LA 70504 (318/231-6553).

MAINE
The Jackson Laboratory
Summer Student Program
Features research in mammalian genetics.

CONTACT: Training and Education, The Jackson Lab., 600 Main St., Bar Harbor, ME 04609-1500 (207/288-6000 x1253).

Maine Maritime Academy
Summer Sea Session
Covers all areas of marine science through lectures, labs, and at-sea experiences including sailing and seamanship.
CONTACT: Ocean Institute, Summer Sea Session, Maine Maritime Academy, Castine, ME 04420 (207/326-4311. ext. 211 or 212).

MARYLAND
The Johns Hopkins University
Center for Talented Youth (CTY)
Spotlights courses that span the liberal arts curriculum. Math and science courses include precalculus, calculus, advanced math, chemistry, biology, genetics, astronomy, ecology, paleobiology, and computer science. Provides 5.5 hours class time and two hours of study hall.
CONTACT: The Johns Hopkins University, 2701 N. Charles St Baltimore, MD 21218 (410/516-0337). (Programs also held at Loyola Marymount Univesity, Los Angeles, CA; Skidmore College, Saratoga Springs, NY; Dickinson College, Carlisle, PA; Hamilton College, Clinton, NY and Franklin and Marshall College, Lancaster, PA. Fifth and sixth graders Young Students Program held at Connecticut College, New London, CT; Goucher College, Baltimore, MD and Loyola Marymount University in Los Angeles, CA.)

Western Maryland College
Summer Science Institute
Offers college-credit course in biological science which focuses on the environment.
CONTACT: Admin. Assistant, Biology Department, Western Maryland College, 2 College Hill, Westminster, MD 21157-4390 (410/857-2400).

MASSACHUSETTS
Boston College
Boston College Experience
Provides an unusual opportunity for students to immerse themselves in activities important to them. Introduces students to a campus environment and encourages personal exploration, growth, and discovery of new interests. Helps students develop strategies for dealing with the more intense and unique demands of college study.
CONTACT: Boston College, McGuinn 100, Chestnut Hill, MA 02167 (617/552-3900).

Boston University
Program in Mathematics for Young Scientists (PROMYS)

Focuses on creative math, including number theory and abstract algebra for first-year participants; returning students study dynamical systems and the Riemann zeta function.
CONTACT: PROMYS, Department of Mathematics, Boston University, Boston, MA 02215 (617/353-2563).

Brandeis University (call for additional programs)
Brandeis Summer Odyssey
Features research and courses in physics, astrophysics, biology, biotechnology, chemistry, math, and computer science.
Minority Research Intern Program
Features research in biology, biochemistry, chemistry, physics, psychology, computer science, and math. As part of the Brandeis Summer Odyssey Program, interns participate in all Summer Odyssey activities and have access to university faculty.
CONTACT: Assistant Director, Brandeis Summer Odyssey, P.O. Box 9110, Waltham, MA 02254 (781/736-2111 or 781/736-2000).

Hampshire College
Summer Studies in Mathematics
Features small classes and seminars that actively investigate problems concerning number theory, combinatorics, dynamics, chaos, and topology. The large faculty lives in a program dorm to foster a community in which math is created, shared, and enjoyed.
CONTACT: Summer Studies in Mathematics, Hampshire College, Box NS, Amherst, MA 01002 (413/559-5375).

Harvard University Summer School
Secondary School Students Program
Highlights courses for undergraduate credit in anthropology (including archaeology), astronomy, biochemistry, biology, chemistry, computer science, engineering science, history of science, math (college algebra, graphs, functions and mathematical modeling, precalculus, calculus, multivariable calculus, linear algebra and differential equations), psychology, quantitative reasoning, physics (and laboratory electronics), sociology, statistics.
CONTACT: Secondary School Program, Harvard University, Department 250, 51 Brattle St., Cambridge, MA 02138 (617/495-3192).

Massachusetts Institute of Technology (call for additional programs)
Minority Introduction to Engineering and Science (MITES)
Features courses in calculus, physics, chemistry, biochemistry, writing, and design. Includes lectures, field trips, and cultural and fun trips.

122   Is There an Engineer Inside You?

CONTACT: Director, MITES Program, MIT, 77 Massachusetts Ave., Rm. 1-211, Cambridge, MA 02139 (617/253-8051).

Mount Holyoke College
SummerMath
Highlights courses in the fundamental concepts of math and computer programming, focusing on process and exploration. Features workshops in problem-solving, genetics, psychology, and building confidence in math.
CONTACT: SummerMath, Mount Holyoke College, South Hadley, MA 01075 (413/538-2608).

Northfield Mount Hermon School
Summer School
Features intensive courses for credit or no grade in biology, chemistry, physics, mathematical modeling, archaeology, geometry, algebra, and precalculus.
CONTACT: Director of Summer School, Northfield Mount Hermon School, Northfield, MA 01360-1046 (413/498-3290).

Radcliffe College
Radcliffe Summer Program in Science
Highlights introductory college-level courses and intensive lab work in physics, chemistry, and biochemistry. Includes relevant site visits and career discussions.
CONTACT: Radcliffe Summer Program in Science, 10 Garden St., Cambridge, MA 02138 (617/495-8626).

Smith College
Summer Science Program
Features hands-on research with Smith faculty in biology, chemistry, and physics. Includes career workshops and discussions with women scientists.
CONTACT: Director, Clark Science Center, Smith College, Northampton, MA 01063 (413/585-3879).

Springfield College
Real World Science
A fun mixture of science, field trips, adventure, and problem-solving that emphasizes solving real-world problems. Features human ecology, evolution, behavior, and performance.
CONTACT: Continuing Education, Springfield College, Alden Street, Springfield, MA 01109 (413/748-3111).

Tufts University (call for additional programs)
Adventures in Veterinary Medicine

Features an educational, career exploration program for students interested in careers in veterinary medicine. Offers short courses with Tufts faculty, tours, rotations, and speakers.
CONTACT: Director of Summer/Special Programs, Tufts University, School of Veterinary Medicine, 200 Westboro Road, N. Grafton, MA 01536 (508/627-3454).
Tufts Study
Students select two courses for college credit from more than 40 offered in biology, calculus, astronomy, and physics. Courses are supplemented by workshops, college tours. Introduction to Professions, and recreational activities.
CONTACT: Tufts University Summer School, 112 Packard Ave., Medford, MA 02155 (617/627-3454).

University of Massachusetts at Amherst (call for additional programs)
Engineering Career Orientation
Features four courses in computers, English, math and chemistry. Includes field trips and speakers from the College of Engineering, as well as alumni speakers.
CONTACT: Minority Engineering Program, University of Mass., 128 Marston Hall, Amherst, MA 01003 (413/545-2030).
Northeast Science Enrichment Program
Hands-on activities in chemistry, biology, math, computer science, physics, and language arts. Educational, cultural, and recreational field trips.
CONTACT: Department of Math and Statistics, Lederle Graduate Research Center, University of Massachusetts, Amherst, MA 01003 (413/545-1909).

University of Massachusetts Medical Center
High School Health Careers Program
Offers enrichment classes in the mornings and research apprenticeships in one of UM's many labs.
CONTACT: University Of Massachusetts Medical Center, Office of Science Education, 55 Lake Ave. North, Worcester, MA 01655 (508/856-5541).

Worcester Polytechnic Institute (call for additional programs)
Frontiers in Science, Mathematics, and Engineering
Students select an area of concentration: physics, chemistry, mathematics, biology, electrical and computer engineering, civil engineering, or computer science.
CONTACT: Worcester Polytechnic Institute, Provost Office, 100 Institute Road, Worcester, MA 01609-2280 (508/831-5591).
Strive for College and Careers in Mathematics, Engineering and Science
Features a two-week course in biology, electrical and computer engineering, chemistry, civil engineering, math, computer science, or physics. A two-week research internship follows in the same or different field.

CONTACT: Worcester Polytechnic Institute, Office of Multicultural Affairs, Outreach Programs Office, 100 Institute Road, Worcester, MA 01609-2280 (508/831-5819).

MICHIGAN
Eastern Michigan University
Summer Quest
Features an intense academic experience embedded into a program that addresses not only intellectual challenge, but also interpersonal relationships and personal development. Courses include beginning chemistry, physics, CAD, computer animation, video production, theater workshop, creative writing, and entrepreneurship.
CONTACT: Honors Program, E. Michigan University, Ypsilanti, MI 48197 (313/487-0902).

Hillsdale College
Summer Science Camps
Features hands-on courses in molecular biology or chemistry and physics designed to promote scientific literacy among high school students.
CONTACT: Hillsdale College, Biology Department, Hillsdale, MI 49242 (517/437-7341).

Michigan Technological University (call for additional programs)
American Indian Biological and Computer Science Workshop
Offers participants choice of two different intensive areas of investigation: biology and computer science. Emphasizes individual and small group work to solve problems and discover the wonders of science. Recreational activities include guest speakers, hands-on activities, picnics, athletics, and career-oriented presentations.
Michigan State Board of Education Summer Institute for the Arts, Sciences and Technologies
Features courses in engineering design, creative writing, chemistry, German, physics, and writing for publication.
Minorities in Engineering
Provides an overview of many engineering and related areas such as mechanical, electrical, chemical, civil, geological, metallurgical, and environmental engineering; bioengineering; computer science; engineering technology; mathematics; physics; and career planning.
Summer Youth Program
Provides opportunities for active learning in a variety of fields, such as chemical, civil, mechanical, electrical, and geological engineering; robotics, CAD, medical physiology, microbiology; genetics engineering, programming in Basic; electronics; limnology; mineralogy and field geology; aquatic ecology; mountain biking; theater; creative writing; criminal justice systems; astronomy; architecture; photography, and others.

Women in Engineering
Provides an overview of many engineering and related areas such as bioengineering, chemical, civil, electrical, geological, mechanical, metallurgical, and environmental engineering; applied technology; mathematics; physics; and career planning.
CONTACT: Youth Programs Office, Michigan Tech. University, 1400 Townsend Dr., Houghton, MI 49931 (906/487-2219).

University of Michigan
Summer Engineering Academy (SEA)
Offers a series of classes in engineering enrichment and exposure. Program components incorporate math, computer, and communications classes; research; and personal development.
CONTACT: Director, Engineering Industrial Support Program, University of Michigan, 2316 EECS Bldg., 1301 Beal Ave., Ann Arbor, MI 48109-2116 (734/764-6497 or 734/764-1817).

MINNESOTA
Carleton College
Introduction to Mathematical and Scientific Reasoning
Features courses in chemistry, physics, computer graphics, astronomy, aquatic biology, field geology, computer modeling, and mathematical reasoning.
CONTACT: Summer Academic Programs, Carleton College, One North College St., Northfield, MN 55057 (507/663-4153).

Macalester College
Minnesota Institute for Talented Youth (MITY)
Provides challenging courses in science and math including physics, chemistry, animal behavior, DNA literacy, field biology, astronomy, trigonometry, geometry and fractals, and creative math. Also offers classes in the dramatic and visual arts, music performance, social sciences, foreign languages, humanities, and writing.
CONTACT: Director, Minnesota Inst. for Talented Youth, 1600 Grand Ave., c/o Macalester College, St. Paul, MN 55105 (612/696-6590).

University of Minnesota, Morris (call for additional programs)
Biotechnology and Human Reproduction: Tinkering with Nature
Examines the new techniques of biological sciences used to tinker with human reproduction.Covers biology, public policy, genetics, and philosophy.
Summer Education Experience
Features college-level scientific research and activities including lab safety and technology, independent research, discussions of ethical perspectives on scientifc inquiry, and career exploration in the sciences.

CONTACT: Continuing Education and Summer Session, 231 Community Services Bldg, University of Minnesota, Morris, MN 56267 (320/589-2211).

MISSISSIPPI
Jackson State University (call for additional programs)
Allied Health Pre-Health Program
Features intensive courses for students interested in allied health careers. Subjects include biology, college algebra, chemistry, math, test-taking, and hearing skills.
Minority High School Students Research Apprentice Program
Students conduct research in JSU scientists' labs on a health-related project. CONTACT: Jackson State University, School of Science and Tech., Health Careers Office, P.O. Box 18780, 1400 J.R. Lynch St, Jackson, MS 39206 (601/968-2202).
Summer Science Camps
Intensive course work and lab experiments under the guidance of mentors expose students to the natural sciences, math, communication skills, and computer science through individual and group studies. Includes speakers and field trips.
CONTACT: JSU, Department of Mathematics, Jackson, MS 39217 (601/ 973-3449).

NEBRASKA
University of Nebraska-Lincoln
Biology Career Workshop
Features hands-on instruction in applied and basic life sciences. Activities include involvement with UNL faculty on field projects and lab experiences, workshops on career opportunities, and informational sessions about college admissions and scholarships.
CONTACT: University of Nebraska, 103 Ag. Hall, P.O. Box 830702, Lincoln, NB 68583-0702 (402/472-2541).

NEW HAMPSHIRE
Phillips Exeter Academy
Phillips Exeter Academy Summer School
Features courses in algebra (all levels), geometry (all levels), trigonometry, precalculus, logic, probability, problem-solving, computer science, chemistry (all levels), genetics, physiology, astronomy, astrophysics, oceanography, physics (all levels), and advanced biology.
CONTACT: Phillips Exeter Academy, Summer School Admissions, Exeter, NH 03833 (603/772-4311 ext. 3488). Please call for catalogue.

NEW JERSEY
Drew University, Madison - College Gifted Programs
The Summer Institute for the Gifted (Co-ed)

College professors teach challenging academic courses in number theory, problem solving and critical thinking, algebra, P/SAT math, geometry, precalculus/ trigonometry, PASCAL, biology, chemistry, space technology, robotics, veterinary medicine, anatomy and physiology, physics, archaeology, humanities, ethics, and arts. Many recreational and cultural activities also are available. **CONTACT:** College Gifted Programs, 120 Littleton Road, Ste. 201, Parsippany, NJ 07054-1803 (973/408-3000). (See also College Gifted Programs at George Schol, Newtown, and Bryn Mawr College, Bryn Mawr, PA; and Vassar College in Poughkeepsie, NY).

Cook College, Rutgers - The State University of New Jersey (call for additional programs)
Discovery - An Academic Enrichment and Apprenticeship Program in Science and Technology
Offers faculty-sponsored research apprenticeships in biological, marine, and environmental sciences; engineering; and science education, as well as courses in math, English, and computer science.
CONTACT: Rutgers University, Cook College, Martin Hall, Rm. 109-B, P.O. Box 231, New Brunswick. NJ 08903 (732/932-9650 or 732/932-1766).

Douglass College of Rutgers, The State University of New Jersey
Douglass Science Institute Program Series
The 9th grade component introduces biology, chemistry, physics, computers, and mathematics through "hands-on" labs and workshops. The 10th grade component highlights biology and chemistry. Students who participate in the 9th grade program will be eligible to apply for the 10th grade program the following year.
CONTACT: Program Coord., Douglass Project for Rutgers Women in Math, Science, and Engineering, Douglass College, P.O. Box 270, New Brunswick, NJ 08903-0270 (732/932-9197).

Drew University
New Jersey Governor's School in the Sciences
Highlights a core curriculum in physics, chemistry, biology, math, and computer science. Features hands-on labs and team projects, field trips, and evening colloquia designed to introduce scientific research, present career options, and broaden appreciation and knowledge of science.
CONTACT: NJ high school gidance counselor.

New Jersey Institute of Technology (call for additional programs)
Summer Academy in Technology and Science
Offers up to eight college credits in small, customized classes taught by faculty.
CONTACT: Precollege Programs, NJ Institute of Technology, University Heights, Newark, NJ 07102 (973/596-3679 or 973/596-3000).

Rutgers University (call for additional programs)
The Engineering Experience for Minorities (T.E.E.M.)
Immerses students into the world of engineering through research projects, classes in scientific methdology, communications, electronics and computers, lab work, plant tours, and workshops. Emphasizes team and small group work.
CONTACT: Rutgers College of Engineering, P.O. Box 909, Office of Special Programs, Rm. B-110, Piscataway, NJ 08855-0909 (732/932-2687).

NEW MEXICO
New Mexico Tech (call for additional programs)
Mini Courses
Introduces research and course work in science, engineering, and business. May offer programs in environmental science or engineering, mineral and materials engineering, business administration, and computer science. Includes lectures, labs, and field trips to relevant industries and research sites.
CONTACT: New Mexico Tech, Office of Admissions, Campus Station, Socorro, NM 87801 (505/835-5424 or 800/4288324 x1).

NEW YORK
Barnard College/Columbia University
Summer in New York: A Pre-College Program
Features a college-level liberal arts program for bright, motivated students. Courses include math and math theory, psychology, environmental science, economics, statistics, biology, and humanities.
CONTACT: Director of Summer New York Pre-College Programs, Barnard College/Columbia University, 3009 Broadway, New York, NY 10027-6598 (212/854-8866).

Pace University (call for additional programs)
Physiology and Biochemistry of Microorganisms
Introduces students to basic microbial techniques followed by identification of bacteria. Enrichment media are used to detect enzyme activity and product formation. Advanced students are involved in hereditary unit transfer, plasmid incorporation, and DNA cuts with endonucleases.
CONTACT: Department of Biological Science, Pace University, 1 Pace Plaza, NY, NY 10038 (212/346-1504).

Pace University, Pleasantville
Science Studies .for High Ability High School Students
Features regularly scheduled classes in chemistry, general biology, physics, nutrition, astronomy, human biology, and others.
CONTACT: Pace University, Pleasantville, NY 10570 (914/773-3718).

Rensselaer Polytechnic Institute
High School Summer Program
Highlights courses in architecture, chemistry, computing, management, math, physics, psychology, rhetoric and writing, and science and technology studies.
CONTACT: Rensselaer Polytechnic Institute, Office of Undergraduate Admissions, Troy, NY 12180-3590 (518/276-6370; 800/448-6562).

Skidmore College
Adirondack Life Science Institute
An intensive program that introduces the various subdisciplines within the life sciences including Molecular Biology, Cell Biology, Genetics Ecology, Bioethics, and Medicine.
CONTACT: Department of Biology, Skidmore College, Saratoga Springs, NY 12866 (518/584-5000).

State University of New York
Summer Science Camp and Math/Science Career Access Clubs
Offers a campus-based, school-based, and community-based approach to science, engineering, and math exploration through classes, research, experiments, field trips, informal workshops, club activities, and recreation. The four-week residential program is offered to rising 8th grade students. There is an academic year follow-up during 9th grade. Academic year club activities are offered on a weekly basis for 7th and 8th grade students, and are facilitated by advisors. Club participants develop science projects, learn new technology, attend lectures, demonstrations, and plan relevant field trips. Features a year-end science fair.
CONTACT: State University of New York, Department of Tech. and Society, Stony Brook, NY 11794-2250 (516/632-8761).

State University of New York, Oneonta
Bio 108. Ecology and Field Biology
Introduces the ecology of terrestrial and freshwater habitats of the supper Susquehanna River Basin.
CONTACT: Director, State University of New York Oneonta Biological Field Station, RD2, Box 1066, Cooperstown, NY 13326 (607/547-8778).

Stuyvesant Institute at New York Institute of Technology (call for additional programs)
Summer Research Program (STS)
Feaures STS research in the biological sciences, physical and mathematical sciences, medical sciences, engineering an applied sciences, and behavioral and social sciences. Includes individual study and research projects super-

vised by university, national laboratory, private research institute, and private corporate staff and faculty.
CONTACT: Stuyvesant Institute (STS), Bowling Green Station, P.O. Box 843, New York, NY 10274 (212/747-1755; 800/292-4452). (Programs also held in Russia, Asia, South America, and Europe.)

Syracuse University
Summer College Engineering
Highlights courses in physics, chemistry, biology, math, PASCAL, and precalculus.
CONTACT: Syracuse University, Division of Summer Sessions, Ste. 230, 111 Waverly Ave., Syracuse, NY 13244-2320 (315/443-5294).

United States Military Academy
Invitational Academic Workshop
Students choose four of fourteen workshops in basic and applied science or the humanities.
CONTACT: United States Military Academy, 606 Thayer Road, West Point, NY 10996 (914/938-4041).

University at Stony Brook, State University of New York
Simony Fellowship Program
Provides research opportunities in all sciences.
CONTACT: Undergraduate Studies, Library E3320, State University of New York, Stony Brook, NY 11794 (516/632-7080).

NORTH CAROLINA
Davidson College
Davidson July Experience
An educational, social, creative, and self-developing program in which students choose two courses taught by Davidson professors from seven liberal arts disciplines.
CONTACT: Director, Davidson July Experience, Education Department, Davidson College, Davidson, NC 28036 (704/892-2130).

Duke University (call for additional programs)
Duke Action: Science Camp for Young Women
Focuses on the behaviors of and interactions between living things and their environments, as well as the human impact on the environment. Instruction in forest and marine environments integrates biological and physical sciences with writing, the arts, and social sciences. Features interaction with women role models.
CONTACT: Youth Programs, Office of Continuing Education, Duke University, Box 90702, Durham, NC 27708 (919/684-6259).

PreCollege Program
Students select two courses from a wide range of introductory-level undergrad courses, some of which include astronomy, biology, calculus, engineering, computer science, chemistry, and physics. Courses taught by Duke faculty and open to undergrads. Speakers, seminars, and tours also are offered.
CONTACT: Coordinator, Precollege Programs, P.O. Box 90747, Duke University, Durham, NC 27708-0747 (919/683-1725).

TIP Scientific Field Studies
Advanced scientific seminars involving field work in unique research settings. Focuses on hands-on development of scientific skills. Previous courses have included marine biology (NC, TX), mountain ecology (CO, VA),aquaculture (HI), and an international study program in tropical ecology (Costa Rica).
CONTACT: TIP Scientific Field Studies, P.O. Box 90747, Duke University, Durham, NC 27708-0747 (919/684-3847).

TIP Summer Residential Program
Features courses in chemistry, physics, astronomy, bioethics, marine biology, animal behavior, psychology, logic, computer science, precalculus, math problem-solving, number theory, and environmental studies.
CONTACT: Duke University Talent Identification Program, P.O. Box 90747, Duke University, Durham, NC 27708-0747 (919/684-3847).

University of North Carolina (call for additional programs)
Summer Ventures in Science and Mathematics (SVSM)
Features courses and research in natural and physical sciences, math, computer science, career exploration, communications skills needed for competitions, and social issues related to science.
CONTACT: Summer Ventures in Science and Mathematics, P.O. Box 2976, Durham, NC 27715 (919/286-3366, x523). (Program held on six campuses: Appalachian State University, East Carolina University, North Carolina Central University, UNC-Charlotte, UNC-Wilmington, and Western Carolina University).

OHIO
College of Mount Saint Joseph
Women in Science and Mathematics
In a workshop environment, participants work with women scientists in biology, chemistry, physics, geology, anthropology, and math to explore career opportunities.
CONTACT: Department of Biology, College of Mount St. Joseph, Cincinnati, OH 45233 (513/244-4411).

Denison University
Investigations in the Sciences

Features brief, active research experiences with faculty in astronomy, biology, chemistry, math, and psychology. Includes field trips in geology and archaeology. Highlights choice of two disciplines for intensive hands-on work.
CONTACT: Denison University, Granville, OH 43023 (740/587-6677).

Miami University
Junior Scholars Program
Program offers college credit and campus living for academically talented high school students. Disciplines include math, computer science, biology, physics, geology, social sciences, humanities, languages, and fine arts.
CONTACT: Jr. Scholars Program, Miami University, Oxford, OH 45056 (513/529-5818).

Ohio Academy of Science
B-WISER Institute: Buckeye Women in Science, Engineering, and Research
Enhances interest in physics, chemistry, biology, geological science, and math. Consists of three activities: a summer camp, year-long internships, and a career workshop.
CONTACT: Ohio Academy of Science, 1500 W. 3rd Ave., Ste. 223, Columbus, OH 43212-2817 (614/488-2228).

Ohio State University
Ross Young Scholars Program
Offers a ground-breaking program for students who have a strong desire to pursue careers in math, science, or technology. To provide a vivid apprenticeship to research.
CONTACT: Department of Math, Ohio State University, 231 West 18th Ave., Columbus, OH 43210 (614/292-1569).

Ohio University
Pre-Engineering Programs for Minorities (PEP)
Features course work in precalculus, engineering, and study skills.
CONTACT: PEP, College of Engineering and Tech., Ohio University, Athens, OH 45701 (740/593-1482).

OKLAHOMA
University of Oklahoma
Minority High School Student Research Apprentice Program
Offers a full-time research experience in biomedical research and health professions. Also awards grants to teachers who are either members o a minority or teach minority students.
CONTACT: Office of the Provost, University of Oklahoma, 650 Parrington Oval, Rm. 100, Norman, OK 73019-0390 (405/325-3521).

OREGON
Lewis and Clark College
Summer College Exploration
Exposes students to all aspects of college life, including classes, residence halls, information resources, and outside activities. Offers classes in natural science, social science, fine arts, and humanities.
CONTACT: Summer Coord., Campus Box 39, Lewis and Clark College, Portland, OR 97219 (503/768-7297).

PENNSYLVANIA
Camp Watonka, Inc.
Science Camp Watonka
Campers select their own programs, which include daily instruction, labs, and demonstrations in astronomy, biology, chemistry, computer science, earth science, electronics, ham radio, robotics, rocketry, combined with traditional camp activities.
CONTACT: Director, Camp Watonka, P.O. Box 127, Hawley, PA 18428 (717/226-4779).

Carnegie Mellon University (call for additional programs)
Advanced Placement Early Admission
Features courses in physics, chemistry, biology, history, English, computing, calculus, and discrete math.
CONTACT: Director of Summer Studies, Summer Studies Office, Carnegie Mellon University, 5000 Forbes Ave., Pittsburgh, PA 15213-3890 (412/268-6620).
Pennsylvania Governor's School for the Sciences
Features research and courses in biology, chemistry, physics, math, and computer science.
CONTACT: Carnegie Mellon University, Doherty Hall 2201, Schenley Park, PA 15213 (412/268-6669)

Lebanon Valley College
Daniel Fox Youth Scholars Institute
Offers programs in animal physiology, chemistry, experimental, genetics, math. computer science, physics, psychobiology, psychology (experimental and clinical), sound recording technology, and sociology.
CONTACT: Biology Department, Lebanon Valley College, Annville, PA 17003 (717/867-6213).

Penn State University and the Penn. Department of Education
Pennsylvania Governor's School for the Agricultural Sciences (PGSAS)

Features research and courses in science, food technology and policy, and agriculture and natural resources.
CONTACT: PSU, College of Agricultural Sciences, 101 Agricultural Admin. Bldg, University Park, PA 16802 (814/865-7521).

Penn State University (call for additional programs)
Summer Space Academy
Provides research internships in many different space-related research projects in engineering and the physical and life sciences. Features lectures and discussions on research and its social context.
CONTACT: PSU, 102 S. Frear Lab, University Park, PA 16802 (814/863-7688).
Women in Engineering (WIE) Week
Features hands-on labs, guest speakers, and a design contest.
CONTACT: Penn State University, 101 Hammond Bldg., University Park, PA 16802 (814/865-3342).

Seton Hill College (call for additional programs)
Science-Quest
A hands-on program for girls featuring collaborative learning. Includes indoor and outdoor scientific excursions and female role models. Integrates science and math in a cooperative environment.
CONTACT: Office of Continuing Education, Seton Hill College, Greensburg, PA 15601 (724/838-4280).

University of Pennsylvania (call for additional programs)
Penn Summer Science Academy
Offers a choice of concentration in molecular biology, math, or environmental science. Features lab and field projects, and faculty-led problem-solving workshops in current areas of research. Also includes faculty, lectures, discussions and debates on related social and ethical concerns, and visits to research sites.
CONTACT: University of Pennsylvania, Office of Special and Youth Programs, 3440 Market St., Ste. 100, Philadelphia, PA 19104-3335 (215/898-5809).

University of Pittsburgh at Bradford
Young Scientists
Highlights research and courses in chemistry, physics, biology, geology, math, and computer science.
CONTACT: Computer Science, University of Pittsburgh at Bradford, 209 Fisher Hall, 300 Campus Dr., Bradford, PA 16701-2898 (814/362-7542).

TENNESSEE
Christian Brothers University

Early Identification Program (EIP)
An intensive program for high school students from underrepresented groups interested in engineering. Offers courses for college credit in math and engineering design; role and peer motivational experiences.
CONTACT: Director, Early Identification Program for Minorities in Engineering, School of Engineering, Christian Brothers University, 650 E. Parkway South, Memphis, TN 38104 (901/321-3405).

Tennessee Technological University (call for additional programs)
Introduction to Engineering, and Computers Workshop
Participants are enrolled in three courses: "Energy," "FORTRAN 77," and "Introduction to Engineering Design." A series of lectures titled "Introduction to Engineering" is offered as well as tours of industries. Each student completes an assigned research project.
CONTACT:Tennessee Technological University, P.O. Box 5005, Cookeville, TN 38505 (931/372-3172).

TEXAS
Baylor University
High School Summer Science Research Fellowship Program
Provides students hands-on research experience by working on research projects with University professors in science, math, and related fields.
CONTACT: Baylor University, P.O. Box 97286, Waco, TX 76798-7286 (254/710-3437 or (254/710-1011).

The Hockaday School
Careers in Technology: An Introduction to Technologically Oriented Fields for Girls
Explores career opportunities in math and science related fields through hands-on experiences and field trips, aswell as through presentations by many female professionals in fields such as medicine, computers, engineering, geology, and financial management.
CONTACT: The Hockaday School, 11600 Welch Road, Dallas, TX 75229-2999 (214/363-6311, FAX: 214/363-0942).

Prairie View A&M University (call for additional programs)
Mathematics and Computer Science Enrichment Experience (MCEE)
Features courses in algebra, trigonometry, and physics. Seminars focus on careers in the various engineering disciplines.
Minority Introduction to Engineering (MITE)
Highlights courses in algebra, trigonometry and physics. Seminars focus on careers in the various engineering disciplines.
Science Careers Opportunity Enhancement (SCOPE)

Offers mini-courses in algebra, trigonometry, computer science, biology, and English.
CONTACT: Career Planning and Outreach Center, Prairie View A&M University, P.O. Box 66, Prairie View, TX 77446-0066 (800/622-9643).

Southern Methodist University (call for additional programs)
College Experience
Provides a head-start on college and a taste of campus life uring an exciting five-week summer program of college-credit courses. Morning classes include philosophy, English, math, psychology, history, anthropology, and government. In the afternoon, all students participate in a "core" or huanities overview class for three hours of college credit. Students who elect to live in the CE residence hall will participate in special cultural, educational, and recreational activities.
TAG
Features two stimulating classes chosen from SMU's wide selection of credit and noncredit courses. Provides cultural enrichment activities for all students. Three-credit courses include mathematical sciences, economics, political science, computer science, psychology, logic, and ethics. Noncredit courses range from literature and writing, music, and theater workshop to anthropology, mechatronics/robotics I and II, computer science, engineering, and environmental science.
CONTACT: Office of Precollege Students, SMU, P.O. Box 382, Dallas, TX 75275-0382 (214/SMU-KIDS).

Southwest Texas State University
Annual SWT Honors Summer Math Camp
Academically talented students participate in this 4-week program. The goal is to excite young students about mathematics.
CONTACT: SWT Honors Summer Math Camp, Department of Mathematics, Southwest Texas State University, San Marcos, TX 79666 (512/245-3439).

Tarleton State University
Advanced Chemistry Applications Program for Talented High School Students
Offers research and course work in chemistry and chemistry applications. Research includes organic, inorganic, and theoretical (computer) components; course work is for college credit.
CONTACT: Department of Physical Sciences, Tarleton State University, Stephenville, TX 76402 (254/968-9143 or 254/968-9000).

Texas A&M University-Galveston
Sea Camp

A five-day adventure that explores the wonders of the marine environment through hands-on activities.
CONTACT: Texas A&M University, P.O. Box 1675, Galveston, TX 77553-1675 (409/740-4525).

Texas Tech University
Clark Foundation Summer Scholars Program
Emphasizes science, math, and engineering; however, all academic disciplines are available.
CONTACT: Department of Biological Sciences, Texas Tech University, Lubbock, TX 79409 (806/742-2715).

Texas Woman's University
Access to Careers in the Sciences (ACES)
Features research and courses possibly including marine biology, anatomy and physiology, zoology, genetics, microbiology, physics, engineering, chemistry, probability and statistics, and logic.
CONTACT: Texas Woman's University, Science and Math Center for Women, P.O. Box 22785, Denton, TX 76204 (940/898-2769).

University of Dallas (call for additional programs)
ACELA: Analytical Chemistry Emphasizing Laboratory Applications
Offers 4-semester-hour college credit course in Analytical Chemistry (Chem 2211-12) emphasizing and comparing both classical and modern instrumental analysis of soil, water, and biological samples.
CONTACT: University of Dallas, 1845 E. Northgate Dr. Irving, TX 75062-4799 (972/721-5374 or 972/721-5000).
John B. O'Hara Chemical Sciences Institute
Offers 8 semester hours of college credit in general chemistry lecture and lab in 9-week summer program.
CONTACT: University of Dallas, 1845 E. Northgate Dr., Irving, TX 75062-4799 (972/721-5000).

UTAH
University of Utah
Hughes Biological Research Program High School Summer Research
Features three weeks training in basic lab procedures for molecular and cellular biology, followed by six weeks of assisting faculty with biological research, often with independent projects.
CONTACT: Hughes Undergraduate Program, 103 Biology Department, University of Utah, Salt Lake City, UT 84112 (801/581-8921; 800/289-7252).

VIRGINIA
George Mason University

EXCEL: Experience College Education and Living
Highlights courses in astronomy, calculus, economics, precalculus, and psychology. Includes workshops in computing time management, handling stress, and student health.
CONTACT: Program Coord., EXCEL, GMU, 4400 University Dr., Fairfax, VA 22030-4444 (703/ 993-2299).

Mary Baldwin College
Programs for the Exceptionally Gifted (PEG)
A unique Program that allows gifted high school students to begin their college education one to four years early while living with peers their own age. Offers majors in biology, chemistry, biochemistry, medical technology, math, math/computer science, and a variety of liberal arts disciplines.
CONTACT: PEG, Mary Baldwin College, Staunton, VA 24401 (540/887-7039 or 540/887-7000).
Young Women in Science
Features choice of two intensive courses in field ecology, biology from molecules to microbes, and natural products; the chemistry of living things. Four hours of college credit for successful completion.
CONTACT: Summer Programs Office, Mary Baldwin College, Staunton, VA 24401 (703/887-7035 or 703/887-7000).

University of Virginia
Minority Introduction to Engineering (MITE)
Acquaints minority students with engineering and sciences at UVA, and informs them about the general requirements and demands of various undergraduate through pre-engineering courses. Students stay in UV dorms, tour the departments of the school of Engineering and visit local engineering companies.
CONTACT: Director For Minority Affairs, Career Services Office, University of Va., School of Engineering and Applied Sciences, A 127 Thornton Hall, Charlottesville, VA 22901 (804/924-3518).

Wallops Island Marine Science Consortium
Marine Science Precollege Summer Program
Features hands-on field work and lab experiences which immerse students in the exciting fields of Marine Biology, Oceanography, Wetlands Ecology, Shark and Dolphin Behavior, and Experimental Ecology. Offers Open water SCUBA certification.
CONTACT: Mark H. Chlebowski, Academic Director, Wallops Island Marine Consortium, Box 16, Enterprise St., Wallops Island, VA 23337 (804/824-5636).

WASHINGTON
Pacific Lutheran University
Summer Scholars Program

Integrates biology, chemistry, human activities, and public responsibilities in its focus on the Puget Sound environment.
CONTACT: Dr. Judah W. Carr Special Academic Programs, Pacific Lutheran University, Tacoma, WA 98447 (253/531-6900).

Seattle University
Project S.P.L.A.S.H.
Features small work groups who perform experiments daily on topics such as fluid flows, waves, and water quantity and quality. Field trips and guest scientists (primarily women) supplement research activities. Includes field experiments at a residential lakeside science camp.
CONTACT: Seattle University, Department of Math, Seattle, WA 98122 (206/296-5931).

University of Washington (call for additional programs)
Technology Camp
Features group activities in environmental science and engineering, including engineering design projects. Exposes students to career options and mentoring experiences.
CONTACT: University of Washington, Department of Materials Science and Engineering, Seattle, WA 99195 (206/543-1115).
U.S. Department of Energy Environmental Management Pre-College Analytical Chemistry (EMPAC) Program
Features university-level analytical chemistry (quantitative analysis) for university credit; includes lecture and lab.
CONTACT: Department of Chemistry, BG- 10, University of Washington, Seattle, WA 98195 (206/543-8621).

WEST VIRGINIA
West Virginia Wesleyan College
Summer Gifted Program
Includes lectures and labs in physics, math, and computer science, as well as lectures and discussions in creative writing and world history.
CONTACT: West Virginia Wesleyan College, Box 89, Buckhannon, WV 26201 (304/473-8062 or 8314).

WISCONSIN
Lawrence University
Summerscience: Anthropology, Biology, Chemistry, Geology, Mathematics, Psychology
Student selects from one of six areas of concentration for intensive science experience; includes independent lab work, field trips, classroom lectures, problem sessions, and research assignments. Planned evening and weekend recreational activities.

CONTACT: Lawrence University, P.O. Box 599, Appleton, WI 54912 (800/227-0982).

Marquette University (call for additional programs)
Summer Science Camps
Hands-on discoveries and demonstrations in civil, mechanical, electrical, and computer engineering. Students construct a LEGO/TC robot to accomplish a task of their choice. Features career exploration, college planning, and personal development to inform and motivate students for careers in science, engineering, and math.
CONTACT: Marquette University, Upward Bound Project, Milwaukee, WI 53233 (414/288-7368).

Milwaukee School of Engineering (call for additional programs)
Summer Electrical Engineering Program for High School Students
Explores four areas of electrical engineering through hands-on lab projects.
CONTACT: Admissions, Department of Enrollment Management, Milwaukee School of Engineering, 1025 N. Broadway, Milwaukee, WI 53202 (414/277-7200).

University of Wisconsin, Superior
Youth Summer
Features precollege career exploration in veterinary medicine, aerospace, fish biology, botany, medical careers and technology, physical geology, and aquatic ecology, as well as extensive arts and humanities programs.
CONTACT: Youth Summer Office, University of Wisconsin, Main 203-B, Superior, WI 54880 (715/394-8173).

WYOMING
Teton Science School (call for additional programs)
Field Ornithology
Research-oriented field course focuses on the diverse and spectacular world of birds using various field studies.
Wildlife Ecology
A research-oriented field course focuses on wildlife resources management and the basic techniques of field research.
Winter Ecology
Features lectures and field lab on winter ecology, animal adaptations, and behavior.
CONTACT: Teton Science School, P.O Box 68, Kelly, WY 83011 (307/733-4765).

Engineering Societies

The following societies are engineering related. Not every society caters specifically to engineers although engineers are involved in all of them. The societies listed are meant only to be a guide to aid your search for engineering education preparation tools, and this database is not comprehensive. Some fields overlap, so, if you are searching for a particular society, be sure to check under all available disciplines. For example, if you are interested in finding a materials engineering society, you would look under both chemical, civil, and mechanical engineering.

Biomedical Engineering

American Society for Healthcare Engineering (ASHE)
c/o American Hospital Association
1 North Franklin Street Suite 2700
Chicago, IL 60606
312-422-3800
http://www.ashe.org/
ASHE is an organization for facilities managers, engineers, clinical engineering/medical equipment managers, and professionals in the fields of health care design, construction, and safety.

Association for the Advancement of Medical Instrumentation (AAMI)
3330 Washington Blvd., Ste 400
Arlington, VA 22201
800-332-2264
http://www.aami.org/
AAMI is a unique alliance of users and manufacturers of medical instrumentation and technology united in their dedication to the safe use of medical technology.

Biomedical Engineering Society (BMES)
P.O. Box 2399
Culver City, CA 90231
310-618-9322
http://mecca.mecca.org/BME/BMES/society/bmeshm.html
The purpose of the Society is to promote the increase of biomedical engineering knowledge and its utilization.

Society for Biomaterials (SFB)
6518 Walker St., Ste 150
Minneapolis, MN 55426
612-927-8108
http://www.biomaterials.org/
The SFB is a professional society that promotes advances in all phases of materials research and development by encouragement of cooperative educational programs, clinical applications, and professional standards in the biomaterials field.

Rehabilitation Engineering and Assistive Technology Society of North America (RESNA)
1700 North Moore Street, Suite 1540
Arlington, VA 22209-1903
(703) 524-6686
http://www.resna.org/
RESNA is an interdisciplinary association for the advancement of rehabilitation and assistive technologies (AT).

Chemical Engineering Societies
American Chemical Society (ACS)
1155 16th St. NW
Washington, DC 20036
800-227-5558
http://www.acs.org/
The society is recognized as a world leader in fostering scientific education and research, and promoting public understanding of science.

American Institute of Chemical Engineers (AIChE)
345 E. 47th Street
New York, NY 10017
212-705-7338
http://www.aiche.org/
AIChE promotes excellence in chemical engineering education and global practice.

Technical Divisions within the AIChE
Catalysis and Reaction Engineering
The Catalysis and Reaction Engineering division promotes research, development, and the application of cataysis and reaction engineering.

Computing and Systems Technology (CAST)
CAST promotes the application of mathematical and computing principles in all areas of chemical engineering.

Engineering and Construction Contracting
AIChE's Engineering and Construction Contracting Division explores and facilitates the engineering and construction process and develops the understanding between owners, contractors, and suppliers.

Environmental
AIChE's largest division focuses on the application of chemical engineering to solve environmental problems through the design and operation of processing plants and through research and development of equipment and processes.

Food, Pharmaceutical, and Bioengineering
AIChE's Food, Pharmaceutical, and Bioengineering Division encourages increased emphasis on biological sciences in engineering curricula and promotes a better understanding and application of sanitary design principles for process equipment and production.

Forest Products
Members of AIChE's Forest Products Division investigate and disseminate information in the science and technology of the forest products industry as it relates to the chemical engineering environment.

Fuels and Petrochemicals
AIChE's Fuels and Petrochemicals Division was established to further the application of chemical engineering principles in the fields of fuels and petrochemicals.

Heat Transfer and Energy Conversion
AIChE's Heat Transfer and Energy Conversion Division encouragesthe investigation and dissemination of knowledge in the field.

Management
AIChE's Management Division develops communication between practicing engineers and managers and encourages chemical engineering-oriented management training.

Materials Engineering and Sciences
AIChE's Materials Engineering and Sciences Division provides the focal point within AIChE for engineers concerned with materials.

Nuclear Engineering
AIChE's first established division provides a focal point for chemical engineers concerned with the many phases of nuclear chemical engineering, especially the management and treatment of radioactive waste and spent nuclear fuel.

Safety and Health
AIChE's Safety and Health Division 1) furthers the application of chemical engineering to the broad field of safety and health; 2) provides a forum for chemical engineers and others to exchange information concerning all facets of safety and health; 3) acts as a source of information for chemical engineers not actively engaged in safety and health, and alerts them to the importance of the field; and 4) addresses problems of safety and health, and the protection of property in the manufacture and use of chemicals.

Separations
AIChE's Separations Division provides a focal point for members interested in both currently used and novel methods of separations.

Electrochemical Society (ECS)
10 S. Main Street
Pennington, NJ 08534
609-737-1902
http://www.electrochem.orgecs.html
ECS is an international educational, non-profit organization concerned with a broad rnge of phenomena related to electrochemical and solid state science and technology.

National Organization for the Professional Advancement of Black Chemists and Chemical Engineers (NOBCChE)
Howard University
525 College Avenue
Washington, DC 20059
800-776-1419
http://www.imall.com/stores/nobcche/
NOBCChE is committed to the professional and educational growth of underrepresented minorities in the sciences.

American Ceramic Society (ACerS)
P.O. Box 6136
Westerville, OH 43086-6136
614-890-4700
http://www.acers.org/
ACerS is an internatinal association that provides the latest technical, scientific, and educatonal information to its members and others in the ceramics and related materials fields.

American Hydrogen Association (AHA)
1739 West 7th Avenue
Mesa, AZ 85202-1906
800-HYDROGEN
http://www.clean-air.org/
The AHA is a non-profit association of individuals and institutions, technical and non-technical, who are dedicated to the advancement of inexpensive, clean, and safe hydrogen energy systems.

Association of Energy Engineers (AEE)
4025 Pleasantdale Rd., Ste. 420
Atlanta, GA 30340
770-447-5083
http://www.aeecenter.org/
AEE is committed to helping increase energy efficiency, utilize innovative energy service options, enhance environmental management programs, upgrade facility operations, improve equipment performance, as well as bolster their bottom-lines.

Civil Engineering Societies

American Society of Civil Engineers (ASCE)
1801 Alexander Bell Drive
Reston, VA 20191-4400
(703) 295-6350
http://www.asce.org/
ASCE advances professional knowledge and improves the practice of civil engineering.

Technical Divisions within the ASCE

Aerospace (AS)
AS serves those who apply the art of civil engineering to the exploration and development of the space frontier and other extreme environments.

Air Transport (AT)
AT advances the practice of civil engineering and other disciplines affecting air transportation and its support facilities.

Architectural Engineering (AE)
AE provides a forum within the Society for members to consider technical and professional issues related to the art and science of building design, and to provide an opportunity for the public to better understand the important role of the civil engineer in the building design industry.

Construction Division (CD)
CD advances the science of construction engineering projects; to define construction terms and establish construction standards; to harmonize construction practices with design theories; to encourage education and research in construction engineering and management.

Energy (EY)
EY promotes the integrated planning and management of efficient energy systems consistent with social, economic, and environmental objectives and constraints.

Engineering Mechanics (EM)
EM fosters activity and development in applied mechanics and other basic branches of knowledge which form the background and foundation of the civil engineering profession.

Environmental Engineering (EE)
EE advances scientific knowledge and promotes sound engineering thought and practice in the solution of problems of environmental sanitation, notably in the provision of safe, palatable, and ample public, private, and industrial water supplies.

Geomatics (GM)
GM provides leadership within the engineering profession in the fields of surveying, cartography, and integrated geographic information systems.

Highway (HW)
HW advances the science of civil engineering in the administrative, functional, and environmental aspects of highway transportation systems.

Materials Engineering (MT)
MT establishs a means by which the civil engineering profession will be informed of the technology developments in construction materials and provides a forum for the technical advancement of engineers who deal with construction materials.

Pipeline (PL)
PL is a source of information for pipeline technology and professional activities relative to the transmission of liquids, gases, or solids by pipelines.

Urban Planning and Development (UP)
UP advances the art and science of civil engineering by (1) improving the civil engineer's understanding of participation in planning; (2) promoting coordinated planning and programming of public works and private development; (3) emphasizing environmental, social, and economic factors in planning the use and development of land and natural resources; (4) working with other technical divisions of the Society in demonstrating the interrelationships between their concerns and planning and development; and (5) fostering education and research in planning and its relationship to civil engineering.

Urban Transportation (UT)
UT advances the art and science of urban transportation engineering.

Water Resources Engineering (WE)
WE advances and disseminates scientific and engineering knowledge and promotes sound engineering practice by fostering technical activities in all areas of water resources engineering, including hydraulics, hydrology, irrigation, and drainage.

Water Resources Planning and Management (WR)
WR advances and disseminates knowledge in the planning and management of all phases of water resources by emphasizing interdisciplinary and multiple-purpose approaches to planning and management of water resources.

Waterways, Ports, Coastal, and Ocean Engineering (WW)
WW advances and disseminates engineering knowledge concerning the utilization of waterways, ports, harbors, and the oceans and the protection and development of coastal areas, including environmental aspects pertaining thereto.

Institutes of the ASCE
The Geo-Institute of the ASCE
1801 Alexander Bell Drive
Reston, VA 20191-4400
Telephone: (703) 295-6350
http://www.asce.org/geo_inst/index.html
The mission of the Geo-Institute is to integrate the talents and perspectives of individual geo-professionals.

Structural Engineering Institute (SEI) of the ASCE
http://www.asce.org/sei/index.html
SEI serves and promotes the worldwide structural engineering profession and structural-related industry.

Environmental and Water Resources Institute of the ASCE - (EWRI)
http://www.asce.org/gsd/eri/ewri.html
EWRI serves the technical, educational and professional needs of members and the public devoted to the use, conservation, and protection of the global international resources.

ASCE Foundation
Suite 600
1015 15th Street NW
Washington, DC 20005-2606
202-789-2874
http://www.asce.org/instfound/foundation.html
ASCE's mission is to generate resources for the civil engineering profession.

American Concrete Institute (ACI)
P.O. Box 9094
Farmington Hills, MI 48333
248-848-3700
http://www.aci-int.org/
ACI International is dedicated to improving the design, construction, manufacture, and maintenance of concrete structures.

American Institute of Steel Construction (AISC)
1 E. Wacker Dr. Suite 3100
Chicago, IL 60601-2001
312-670-2400
http://www.aisc.org/
AISC's purpose is to expand the use of fabricated structural steel through research and development, education, technical assistance, standardization, and quality control.

Construction Specifications Institute (CSI)
601 Madison Street
Alexandria, VA 22314-1791
800-689-2900
http://www.csinet.org/
CSI provides technical information and products, continuing education, professional conferences, and product shows to enhance communication among all the non-residential building design and construction industry's disciplines.

American Architectural Foundation (AAF)
1735 New York Ave. NW
Washington, DC 20006
202-626-7500
http://www.amerarchfoundation.com/

AAF is dedicated to cultivating the public's understanding of architecture and the human experience.

American Institute of Architects (AIA)
1735 New York Ave. NW
Washington, DC   20006
202-626-7300
http://www.aia.org/
AIA research undertakes as its mission to support architectural research and design excellence by identifying the research needs of the architectural discipline, in its broadest and most inclusive sense; by encouraging, facilitating, and supporting research activities which meet these needs; and by disseminating research results.

Association of Iron and Steel Engineers (AISE)
3 Gateway Center, Ste. 1900
Pittsburgh, PA   15222
412-281-6323
http://www.aise.org/
AISE is dedicated to the advancement of technical and engineering phases of the production and processing of iron and steel.

Association of Engineering Geologists (AEG)
323 Boston Post Rd., Ste. 2D
Sudbury, MA   1776
508-443-4639
http://aegweb.org/
Engineering geology is geologic work that is relevant to engineering, environmental concerns, and the public's health, safety, and welfare.

Geological Society of America (GSA)
3300 Penrose Place
Boulder, CO   80301-9140
303-447-2020
http://www.geosociety.org/
GSA provides access to elements that are essential to the professional growth of earth scientists at all levels of expertise and from all sectors of academia, government, business, and industry.

Association for Women Geoscientists (AWG)
4779 126th St. N
White Bear Lake, MN   55110-5910
612-426-3316
http://www.awg.org/
The AWG is dedicated to enhancing opportunities for women in the geosciences.

Earthquake Engineering Research Institute (EERI)
499 14th Street, Ste. 320
Oakland, CA 94612-1902
510-451-0905
http://www.eeri.org/
The EERI is a national, non-profit, technical society of engineers, geoscientists, architects, planners, public officials, and social scientists.

Seismological Society of America (SSA)
El Cerrito Professional Bldg., Ste. 201
El Cerrito, CA 94530
510-525-5474
http://www.seismosoc.org/
SSA is an international association devoted to the advancement of earthquake science.

Environmental Engineering
American Academy of Environmental Engineers (AAEE)
130 Holiday Ct., No. 100
Annapolis, MD 21401
410-266-3311
http://www.enviro-engrs.org/
AAEE is dedicated to improving the practice, elevating the standards, and advancing the cause of environmental engineering.

American Water Resources Association (AWRA)
950 Hemdon Pky, Ste. 300
Herdon, VA 22070-5528
703-904-1225
http://www.awra.org/
The mission of the AWRA is to promote understanding of water resources and related issues by providing a multidisciplinary forum for education, professional development, and information exchange.

Electrical/Electronic Engineering Societies
Institute of Electrical and Electronics Engineers (IEEE)
345 E. 47th Street
New York, NY 10017
212-705-7900
http://www.ieee.org/
The technical objectives of the IEEE focus on advancing the theory and practice of electrical, electronics and computer engineering and computer science.

Technical Societies within the IEEE

IEEE Aerospace and Electronic Systems Society (AESS)
Measurement and Control Engineering Research Center
College of Engineering
Idaho State University
Pocatello, Idaho 83209-8060
208-236-2307
http://www.ieee.org/society/aes.html
AESS focuses on the design, development, analysis, integration, test, and operation of complex systems, usually utilizing electromagnetic sensors.

IEEE Antennas and Propagation Society
http://www.ieee.org/society/ap.html
The society examines experimental and theoretical advances in antennas including design and development; in the propagation of electromagnetic waves including scattering, diffraction, and interaction with continuous media; and applications pertinent to antennas and propagation, such as remote sensing, applied optics, and millimeter and submillimeter wave techniques.

IEEE Broadcast Technology Society
http://www.ieee.org/society/bt.html
The society focuses on devices, equipment, techniques, and systems related to broadcast technology, including the production, distribution, transmission, and propagation aspects.

IEEE Circuits and Systems Society (CSS)
http://www.ieee-cas.org/
CSS addresses the theory, analysis, design (computer-aided design), and practical implementation of circuits, and the application of circuit theoretic techniques to systems and to signal processing.

IEEE Communications Society (COMSOC)
305 East 47th Street
New York, NY 10017
212-705-7018
http://www.comsoc.org/
COMSOC is a community comprised of a diverse group of industry professionals with a common interest in advancing all communications technologies.

IEEE Components, Packaging, and Manufacturing Technology Society
445 Hoes Lane
P O Box 1331
Piscataway, NJ 08855-1331
732-562-5529
http://www.ieee.org/society/cpmt.html
The society focuses on the scientific, engineering, and production aspects of materials, component parts, modules including hybrids and electronic systems.

IEEE Computer Society (CS)
10622 Los Vaqueros Circle
PO Box 3014
Los Hamitos, CA 90720-1314
714-821-8380
http://www.ieee.org/society/comp.html
The scope of the Society encompasses all aspects of theory, design, practice, and application relating to computer and information processing science and technology.

IEEE Consumer Electronics Society (CES)
http://www.ieee.org/society/ce.html
CES focuses on the consumer-related aspects of leisure, video, and audio electronics; home information and communications systems; and interactive information and display systems.

IEEE Control Systems Society (CSS)
445 Hoes Lane
PO Box 1331
Piscataway. NJ 0885-1331
800-678-
http://www.ieee.org/society/css.html
CSS addresses the theory, design, and application of control systems.

IEEE Dielectrics and Electrical Insulation Society (DEIS)
http://www.ieee.org/society/die.html
The society studies dielectric phenomena and behavior, and development, characterization, and application of all gaseous, liquid, and solid electrical insulating materials and systems utilized in electrical and electronic equipment.

IEEE Education Society
http://www.ieee.org/society/educ.html
The society's interests include educational methods, educational technology, instructional materials, history of science and technology, and educational and professional development programs within the electrical engineering disciplines.

IEEE Electromagnetic Compatibility Society (EMCS)
http://www.ieee.org/society/ec.html
The enhancement of electromagnetic compatibility is the societies focus.

IEEE Electron Devices Society (EDS)
http://www.ieee.org/society/ed.html
The field of interest for EDS is all aspects of the physics, theory, and phenomena of electron and ion devices such as elemental and compound semiconductor devices, quantum effect devices, optical devices, displays and imaging devices, photovoltaics, solid-state sensors and actuators, solid-state power devices, high frequency devices, micromechanics, tubes, and other vacuum devices.

IEEE Engineering in Medicine and Biology Society
National Research Council of Canada
Building M-55 room 382
Ottawa Canada KIA OR8
613-993-4005
http://www.ieee.org/society/emb.html
The society focuses on the application of the concepts and methods of the physical and engineering sciences in biology and medicine.

IEEE Engineering Management Society
http://www.ieee.org/society/em.html
The management sciences and technology applicable to individuals and organizations engaged in or overseeing the management of engineering or technology are concerns, including technology policy development, technology assessment, technology transfer, research, development, design, evaluation, production, commissioning, operation, or decommissioning of technical, electrical or electronic equipment/systems, and allied activities.

IEEE Geoscience and Remote Sensing Society
http://www.ieee.org/society/grs.html
The theory, concepts, and techniques of science and engineering are focused on and apply to sensing the earth, oceans, atmosphere, and space, and the processing, interpretation, and dissemination of this information.

IEEE Industrial Electronics Society (IES)
http://www.ieee.org/society/ie.html
The IES through its members encompasses a diverse range of technical activities devoted to the application of electronics and electrical sciences for the enhancement of industrial and manufacturing processes.

IEEE Industry Applications Society
http://www.ieee.org/society/ia.html
The scope of the Society as a transnational organization is the global development, design, manufacture, and application of electrical systems, apparatus, devices, and controls to the processes and equipment of industry and commerce.

IEEE Information Theory Society
http://www.itsoc.org/
The Society shall strive for the advancement of the theory and practice of electrical engineering and of the allied arts and sciences.

IEEE Instrumentation and Measurement Society (IMS)
http://www.ieee.org/society/im.html
IMS deals with the science of developing and using electrical and electronic instruments for the purpose of measuring, monitoring, or recording various physical phenomena that may or may not be of an electrical nature.

IEEE Lasers and Electro-Optics Society (LEOS)
http://www.ieee.org/society/leos.html
LEOS topics include lasers, optical devices, optical fibers, and associated lightwave technology and their application in systems and subsystems, in which the quantum electronic devices are key elements.

IEEE Magnetics Society (MS)
http://www.ieee.org/society/mag.html
MS is concerned with the treatment of all matters in which the dominant factors are the fundamental developments, design, and certain applications of magnetic devices.

IEEE Microwave Theory and Techniques Society
http://www.ieee.org/society/mtt.html
The society addresses microwave theory, techniques, and applications, as they relate to components, devices, circuits, integrated circuits, multi-circuit assemblies, packages, sub-systems, and systems involving the generation, amplification, processing, modulation, control, transmission, reception, detection, and demodulation of microwave signals.

IEEE Neural Networks Council
http://www.ieee.org/society/nn.html
The field of interest of the Council and its activities and programs shall be the theory, design, application, and development of biologically and linguistically motivated computational paradigms involving neural networks.

IEEE Nuclear and Plasma Sciences Society
http://www.ieee.org/society/nps.html
The fields of interest of the Society are the nuclear and plasma sciences.

IEEE Oceanic Engineering Society
http://www.ieee.org/society/oe.html
All applications of electrical and electronic engineering pertaining to all bodies of water are addressed.

IEEE Power Electronics Society
http://www.ieee.org/society/pel.html
The society deals with the development of power electronics technology.

IEEE Power Engineering Society (PES)
http://www.ieee.org/society/pes.html
The scope of the Society embraces planning, research, development, design, application, construction, installation, and operation of apparatus, equipment, structures, materials, and systems for the safe, reliable, and economic generation, transmission, distribution, conversion, measurement, and control of electric energy.

IEEE Professional Communication Society (PCS)
http://www.ieee.org/society/pc.html
PCS includes the study, development, improvement, and promotion of effective techniques for preparing, organizing, processing, editing, collecting, conserving, teaching, and disseminating any form of technical information by and to individuals and groups by any method of communication.

IEEE Reliability Society (RS)
http://www.ieee.org/society/rel.html
The Society is concerned with the problems involved in attaining reliability, maintaining it through the life of the system or device, and measuring it.

IEEE Robotics and Automation Society
http://www.ieee.org/society/ra.html
Robotics and automation are presented as they are related to robotics.

IEEE Signal Processing Society
http://www.ieee.org/society/sp.html
The society addresses the theory and application of filtering, coding, transmitting, estimating, detecting, analyzing, recognizing, synthesizing, recording, and reproducing signals by digital or analog devices or techniques.

IEEE Social Implications of Technology Society
http://www.ieee.org/society/sit.html
The society deals with the impact of technology on society. The impact of society on the engineering profession. The history of the societal aspects of electrotechnology, and professional, social, and economic responsibility in the practice of engineering and its related technology.

IEEE Solid-State Circuits Council/Society
http://www.ieee.org/society/ssc.html
The society deals with all aspects of solid-state circuits, with emphasis on those aspects which either overlap the present interest of the Member Societies, or are presently not covered by any one Society.

IEEE Systems, Man, and Cybernetics Society (SMCS)
http://www.ieee.org/society/smc.html
SMCS provides analysis and design of biological, ecological, socio-economic, social service, computer information, and operational man-machine systems.

IEEE Ultrasonics, Ferroelectrics and Frequency Control Society
http://www.ieee.org/society/uffc.html
Information is available about the theory, technology, materials, and applications related to ultrasonics, ferroelectrics, and frequency control.

IEEE Vehicular Technology Society (VTS)
http://www.ieee.org/society/vt.html
Information is available about the theoretical, experimental, and operational aspects of electrical and electronics engineering in mobile radio, motor vehicles, and land transportation.

Semiconductor Safety Association (SSA)
1313 Dolley Madison Blvd., Ste. 402
McLean , VA 22101-3926
703-790-1745
http://www2.semiconductorsafety.org/ssa/
SSA is a worldwide organization for safety, health, and environmental professionals.

National Association of Radio and Telecommunications Engineers (NARTE)
P.O. Box 678
Medway, MA 02053
508-533-8333
http://www.narte.org/
NARTE is a professional organization which certifies qualified engineers and technicians in the fields of telecommunications, electromagnetic compatibility/interference, and electrostatic discharge control.

American Association for Artificial Intelligence (AAAI)
445 Burgess Drive
Menlo Park, CA 94025
415-328-3123
http://www.aaai.org/
AAAI aims to increase public understanding of artificial intelligence.

Special Interest Group on Artificial Intelligence (SIGART)
c/o ACM
1515 Broadway, 17th Floor
New York, NY 10036
212-869-7440
http://sigart.acm.org/
SIGART is dedicated to the study of intelligence and its realization in computer systems.

Audio Engineering Society (AES)
60 E. 42nd Street Rm. 2520
New York, NY 10165
212-661-8528
http://www.aes.org/
AES is the only professional society devoted exclusively to audio technology.

Laser Institute of America (LIA)
12424 Research Parkway, Ste. 125
Orlando, FL 32826
407-380-1553
http://www.laserinstitute.org/
LIA is a professional membership society comprised of laser researchers, manufacturers, integrators, and users working together to increase the use and safe application of laser technologies.

Software Engineering Institute
Carnegie Mellon University
Pittsburgh, PA 15213-3890
412-268-5800
http://www.sei.cmu.edu/
The SEI mission is to provide leadership in advancing the state of the practice
of software engineering to improve the quality of systems that depend on
software.

Illuminating Engineering Society of North America (IESNA)
120 Wall Street, 17th floor
New York, NY 10005-4001
212-248-5000
http://www.iesna.org/
IESNA advances knowledge and disseminates information for the improvement of the lighted environment to the benefit of society.

Optical Society of America (OSA)
2010 Massachusetts Ave. NW
Washington, DC 20036
202-223-8130
http://www.osa.org/
The OSA was organized to increase and diffuse the knowledge of optics,
pure and applied; to promote the common interests of investigators of optical
problems, of designers, and of users of optical apparatus of all kinds; and to
encourage cooperation among them.

The International Society for Optical Engineering (SPIE)
P.O. Box 10
Bellingham, WA 98227
206-676-3290
http://www.spie.org/
The society's fundamental mission is to provide world-class education and
information services that enhance and promote the profession and field of
optical engineering and that add quality and value to the careers of the members it serves.

General and Specialty Engineering Societies
American Association of Engineering Societies (AAES)
1111 19th Street NW, Ste. 403
Washington, DC 20036
202-296-2237
http://www.aaes.org/
AAES is a multidisciplinary organization dedicated to advancing the knowledge, understanding, and practice of engineering in the public interest.

Junior Engineering Technical Society (JETS)
1420 King Street Ste 405
Alexandria, VA 22314
888/285-NSPE
http://www.asee.org/jets/
JETS promotes the ethical, competent, and licensed practice of engineering and enhances the professional, social, and economic well-being of its members.

American Consulting Engineers Council (ACEC)
1015 15th St. NW Suite 802
Washington, DC 20005
202-347-7474
http://www.acec.org/
ACEC strives to strengthen the business environment and image of member firms, focusing on quality professional services in a competitive global marketplace.

American Indian Science and Engineering Society (AISES)
5661 Airport BLVD
Boulder, CO 80301
303-939-0023
http://bioc02.uthscsa.edu/aisesnet.html
AISES is a private, non-profit organization which nurtures building of community by bridging science and technology with traditional Native values.

American Society of Plumbing Engineers (ASPE)
3617 E. Thousand Oaks Blvd., No. 210
Westlake Village, CA 91362-3649
805-495-7120
http://www.aspe.org:8080/
ASPE is dedicated to the advancement of the science of plumbing engineering; to the professional growth and advancement of its members; and to the health, welfare, and safety of the public.

National Academy of Engineers (NAE)
2101 Constitution Ave. NW
Washington, DC 20418
202-334-3200
http://www.nae.edu/
The NAE sponsors engineering programs aimed at meeting national needs, encourages education and research, and recognizes the superior achievements of engineers.

International Society for Measurement and Control (ISA)
P.O. Box 12277
Research Triangle Park, NC 27709
919-549-8411
http://www.isa.org/
ISA promotes measurement and control, educating the public about career opportunities and publicizing the field's importance to business and industry.

National Society of Black Engineers (NSBE)
1454 Duke Street
Alexandria, VA 22314
703-549-2207
http://www.nsbe.org/
NSBE's mission is to increase the number of culturally responsible Black engineers who excel academically, succeed professionally, and positively impact the community.

National Society of Professional Engineers (NSPE)
1420 King Street
Alexandria, VA 22314
703-684-2800
NSPE is the only engineering society that represents licensed professional engineers (PEs) across all disciplines.

Society of American Military Engineers (SAME)
P.O. Box 21289
Alexandria, VA 22320
800-336-3097
http://www.penfed.org/allies/al3same.htm
SAME's mission is to bring the Nation's engineers together in peacetime so they can be effectively engaged in emergencies.

Society of Hispanic Professional Engineers (SHPE)
5400 E. Olympic Blvd., Ste. 210
Los Angeles, CA 90022
213-725-3970
http://www.shpe.org/
SHPE promotes the development of Hispanics in engineering, science, and other technical professions to achieve educational excellence, economic opportunity, and social equity.

Society of Motion Picture and Television Engineers (SMPTE)
595 W. Hartsdale Ave
White Plains, NY 10607
914-761-1100
http://www.smpte.org/
SMPTE is an international, award-winning technical society devoted to advancing the theory and application of motion-imaging technology including film, television, video, computer imaging, and telecommunications.

Society of Women Engineers (SWE)
120 Wall Street, 11th floor
New York, NY 10005
212-509-9577
http://www.swe.org/
SWE stimulates women to achieve full potential in careers as engineers and leaders, expands the image of the engineering profession as a positive force in improving the quality of life, and demonstrates the value of diversity.

Society of Fire Protection Engineers (SFPE)
7315 Wisconsin Ave. Suite 1225W
Bethesda, MD 20814
301-718-2910
http://www.sfpe.org/
The purpose of the Society is to advance the science and practice of fire protection engineering and its allied fields, to maintain a high ethical standard among its members, and to foster fire protection engineering education.

American Society of Naval Engineers (ASNE)
1452 Duke St
Alexandria, VA 22314
703-836-6727
http://www.jhuapl.edu/ASNE/
ASNE advances the knowledge and practice of naval engineering in public and private applications and operations, enhances the professionalism and well-being of members, and promotes naval engineering as a career field.

Materials Research Society (MRS)
506 Keystone Drive
Warrendale, PA 15086
724-779-3003
http://www.mrs.org/
MRS is dedicated to goal-oriented basic and applied research on materials of technological importance.

Society for Industrial and Applied Mathematics (SIAM)
3600 University City Science Center
Philadelphia, PA   19104-2688
215-382-9800
http://www.siam.org/
SIAM is dedicated to enriching the profession through publications, conferences, activity groups, and programs.

Society for Mining, Metallurgy, and Exploration (SME)
P.O. Box 625002
Littleton, CO   80162-5002
303-973-9550
http://www.smenet.org/
SME advances the worldwide mining and minerals community through information exchange and professional development.

Society of Naval Architects and Marine Engineers (SNAME)
601 Pavonia Ave.
 Jersey City, NJ   07306
201-798-4800
http://www.sname.org/
SNAME is dedicated to advancing the art, science, and practice of naval architecture, shipbuilding, and marine engineering.

Society of Petroleum Engineers (SPE)
P.O. Box 833836
Richardson, TX   75083-3836
972-952-9393
http://www.spe.org/
SPE's mission is to provide the means to collect, disseminate, and exchange technical information concerning the development of oil and gas resources, subsurface fluid flow, and production of other materials through wellbores for the public benefit; and to provide opportunities through its programs for interested (and qualified) individuals to maintain and upgrade their individual technical competence in these areas.

Society for Pharmaceutical and Medical Device Professionals (ISPE)
3816 W. Linebaugh Ave. Suite 412
Tampa, FL   33624
813-960-2105
http://www.ispe.org/
The society's members are technical professionals who apply their practical knowledge in the regulated pharmaceutical and medical device manufacturing industries.

Society of Plastics Engineers (SPE)
P.O. Box 403
Brookfield, CT 06804-0403
203-775-0471
http://www.4spe.org/
SPE is a network of plastics professionals around the world promoting the knowledge and education of plastics and polymers.

American Society of Safety Engineers (ASSE)
1800 E. Oakton Street
Des Plaines, IL 60018
847-699-2929
http://www.asse.org/
ASSE fosters the technical, scientific, managerial and ethical knowledge, skills, and competency of safety, health, and environmental professionals for the protection of people, property, and the environment; and advances the status and promote the advancement of the safety profession.

American Association for the Advancement of Science (AAAS)
1200 New York Ave. NW
Washington, DC 20005
202-26-6400
http://www.aaas.org/
The society improves public understanding of science.

Association for Women in Science (AWIS)
1200 New York Ave. NW Suite 650
Washington, DC 20005
800-886-AWIS
http://www.awis.org/
The society is dedicated to achieving equity and full participation for women in science, mathematics, engineering, and technology.

National Science Foundation (NSF)
4201 Wilson Blvd.
Arlington, VA 22230
703-306-1070
http://www.nsf.gov/
The NSF is an independent U.S. government agency responsible for promoting science and engineering through programs that invest over $3.3 billion per year in almost 20,000 research and education projects in science and engineering.

National Organization of Gay and Lesbian Scientists and Technical Professionals (NOGLSTP)
P.O. Box 91803
Pasadena, CA 91109
626-791-7689
http://www.noglstp.org/
NOGLSTP is a national organization of gays and lesbians employed or interested in scientific or high technology fields.

Mechanical Engineering
Aeronautical/Aerospace Engineering
Aerospace Education Foundation (AEF)
1501 Lee Hwy
Arlington, VA 22209-1198
800-727-3337
http://www.aef.org/
AEF provides aerospace education to the American people, students, and the men and women of the United States Air Force.

American Astronautical Society (AAS)
6352 Rolling Mill Place Suite 102
Springfield, VA 22152
703-866-0020
http://www.astronautical.org/
AAS is the premier independent scientific and technical group exclusively dedicated to the advancement of space science and exploration in the United States.

American Institute of Aeronautics
and Astronautics (AIAA)
1801 Alexander Bell Drive Suite 500
Reston, VA 20191-4344
703-264-7500
http://www.aiaa.org/
AIAA's primary purpose is to advance the arts, sciences, and technology of aeronautics and astronautics and to foster and promote the professionalism of those engaged in these pursuits.

Experimental Aircraft Association (EAA)
P.O. Box 3086
Oshkosh, WI 54903-3086
920-426-4800
http://www.eaa.org/
EAA is dedicated to serving all of aviation by fostering and encouraging individual participation, high standards, and access to the world of flight in an environment that promotes freedom, safety, family, and personal fulfillment.

National Space Society (NSS)
600 Pennsylvania Ave. SE Suite 201
Washington, DC 20003
202-543-1900
http://www.nss.org/
The NSS promotes change in social, technical, economic, and political conditions to advance the day when people will live and work in space.

Society of Experimental Test Pilots (SETP)
P.O. Box 986
Lancaster, CA 93584
805-942-9574
http://www.netport.com/setp/
SETP strives to broaden professional relationships through the sharing of ideas and experiences which promote and enhance safety, communication, and education.

Maria Mitchell Association (MMA)
2 Vestal Street
Nantucket, MA 02554
508-228-9198
http://www.mmo.org/
MMA strives to increase knowledge and public awareness of the universe and the natural world through programs of scientific research and education.

American Astronomical Society (AAS)
2000 Florida Ave. Suite 400
Washington, DC 20009
202-328-2010
http://www.aas.org/
AAS is a society for astronomers and other scientists and individuals interested in astronomy.

Automotive Engineering
Institute of Transportation Engineers (ITE)
525 School St, SW Ste. 410
Washington, DC 20024-2797
202-554-8050
http://www.ite.org/
ITE members are traffic engineers, transportation planners, and other professionals who are responsible for meeting society's needs for safe and efficient surface transportation through planning, designing, implementing, operating, and maintaining surface transportation systems worldwide.

International Human Powered Vehicle Association (IHPVA)
P. O. Box 1307
San Luis Obispo, CA 93406-1307
805-466-8010
http://www.ihpva.org/
IHPVA is dedicated to promoting improvement, innovation, and creativity
in the design and development of human-powered transportation.

Electric Auto Association (EAA)
2710 St. Giles Lane
Mountain View, CA 94040
800-537-2882
http://www.eaaev.org/
EAA promotes the advancement and widespread adoption of electricity powered automobiles.

Society of Automotive Engineers (SAE)
400 Commonwealth Drive
Warrendale, PA 15096-0001
724-776-4841
http://www.sae.org/
SAE provides technical information and expertise used in designing, building, maintaining, and operating self-propelled vehicles for use on land or
sea, in air or space.

General Mechanical Engineering
American Society of Mechanical Engineers (ASME)
345 E. 47th Street
New York, NY 10017
800-THE-ASME
http://www.asme.org/
ASME promotes and enhances the technical competency and professional well-being
of its members. Through quality programs and activities in mechanical engineering, it
better enables its practitioners to contribute to the well-being of humankind.

Technical Divisions within the ASME
All divisions can be found at the website
http://www.asme.org/ or by contacting the society directly.

Advanced Energy Systems Division
Learn about non-conventional or emerging conversion devices and processes, both direct and indirect.

Aerospace Engineering Division
Information is provided on systems/subsystems, assemblies, and components for highly sophisticated manned and unmanned aerospace applications.

Applied Mechanics Division
Learn about the fundamental and applied field of mechanics, including solids, fluids, shock, vibration, and more.

Bioengineering Division
This division offers information about the division, upcoming meetings and conferences, committee membership, the Journal of Biomechanical Engineering, the division by-laws, and other relevant information.

Design Engineering Division
Information is provided on the concept, development, and design of machines and the mechanical design aspects of other phases of engineering.

Electrical and Electronic Packaging Division
Learn about the technology of electrical and electronic equipment design, development, testing, manufacturing, and applications support.

FACT Division Home Page
Engineers and scientists in combustion, boilers, fuels, coal, oil, natural gas, and environmental control use this home page.

Fluids Engineering Division
Learn about all areas of fluid mechanics, processes and machines, including pumps, turbines, and compressors.

Fluids Power Systems and Technology Systems Division
Information is provided on fluid power component performance within a complete mechanical system and the physical integration of components within a system.

Heat Transfer Division
Learn about the theory and application of heat transfer in equipment and thermodynamic processes related to all fields of mechanical engineering.

ISPS Division
The mechanical engineer interested in the field of information storage and information processing systems, such as scanners, printers, and digital cameras will find useful information here.

Information Storage and Processing Systems Division
Learn about information storage methodologies: electro-mechanical and electronic information storage devices and their manufacture.

Internal Combustion Engine Division
The division is dedicated to the design, development, manufacture, and application of all types of reciprocating combustion engines, including diesel, dual-fuel, and spark-ignited engines.

International Gas Turbine Institute
The Institute is dedicated to providing international forums for the exchange and development of information to improve the design, manufacture, operation, and application of all types of gas turbines and related equipment.

Manufacturing Engineering Division
Information about exciting events and developments in the world of manufacturing is provided.

Materials Division
Information is provided on the properties of materials and the influence of these properties on design consideration in materials selection for engineering structures.

Materials Handling Engineering Division
Information is provided on systems engineering methods which integrate control technology, information technology, and material transport equipment to provide efficient, safe, and economical material handling.

Noise Control and Acoustics Division
Information is provided on application of physical principles of acoustics to the solution of noise control problems, as well as the uses of acoustics in industrial applications.

Non-Destructive Evaluation Engineering Division
Information is provided on the non-destructive evaluation of critical components and in-service inspection in mechanical engineering applications.

Nuclear Engineering Division
Information is provided on design, analysis, development, testing, operation, and maintenance of reactor systems and components, nuclear fusion, heat transport, nuclear fuels technology, and radioactive waste.

Ocean Engineering Division
Information is provided about technology and systems employed in the ocean environment, particularly equipment and vehicles for underwater sea usage.

Offshore Mechanics and Arctic Engineering
Information is provided on identification and development of the most effective offshore and arctic technologies in private and governmental sectors of the industry as well as in research and in academic institutions.

Petroleum Division
Find out about the entire area of petroleum drilling, production, refining, processing, and transportation.

Plant Engineering and Maintenance Division
The Plant Engineering and Maintenance Division focuses on manufacturing: systems, equipment, processes, and facilities. Through creative problem solving, the goal is to make continuous improvements in costs, quality, safety, processes, and operations.

Power Division
The Power Division provides technology transfer information on fossil-fired thermal and hydroelectric power and energy generation systems and usage. Included are utility, industrial, and institutional power plants and their auxiliary equipment.

Pressure Vessels and Piping Division
Find out about the design, fabrication, construction, inspection, operation, and failure prevention of power boilers, heating boilers, pressure vessels, pipelines, pumps, valves, and other pressure-bearing components.

Process Industries Division
The Process Industries Division focuses on the design of systems and machines for heating, cooling, or treating industrial fluids and gases to create products of enhanced value, including the equipment used and the efficient management and control of the processes themselves.

Safety Engineering and Risk Analysis Division
Information is provided on the application of basic engineering principles to human activities and mechanical engineering systems for predicting and controlling occurrences caused by mechanical and/or human failure.

Solar Energy Division
Find out about all aspects of solar-derived energy for mechanical and electrical power generation, including both active and passive solar applications.

Solid Waste Processing Division
Information is provided on the Solid Waste Processing Division and the design, development, construction, and operation of solid waste processing and disposal facilities. The Solid Waste Processing Division also promotes proper management practices for the ultimate disposal of waste materials, including integrated waste management, recycling, waste combustion, ash handling, composting, and resource recovery.

Technology and Society Division
Learn about the Technology and Society Division, the issue of the social responsibility of the engineer, and the impact of technological progress on society. Five committees plan and guide the activities of this division.

Textile Engineering Division
Information is provided on product and process technology improvements to the many aspects of fiber, composite, textile, and apparel manufacturing operations, textile machinery, and instrumentation.

Tribology Division
Information is provided on all aspects of bearing design, lubrication and wear, including the impact of tribological practice on reliability and maintainability, the economic impact of friction and wear, and bearing design technology to systems engineering.

American Society of Agricultural Engineers (ASAE)
2950 Niles Rd.
St. Joseph, MI 49085-9659
616-429-0300
http://asae.org/
A not-for-profit professional and technical organization of members worldwide interested in engineering knowledge and technology for food and agriculture, associated industries, and related resources.

American Society of Heating, Refrigerating and Air-Conditioning Engineers (ASHRAE)
1791 Tullie Cir. NE
Atlanta, GA 30329
800-5-ASHRAE
404-636-8400

http://www.ashrae.org/
The Society is organized for the sole purpose of advancing the arts and sciences of heating, ventilation, air conditioning, and refrigeration for the public's benefit through research, standards writing, continuing education, and publications.

Refrigerating Engineers and Technicians Association (RETA)
c/o Smith-Bucklin Assocs.
401 N. Michigan Ave
Chicago, IL 60611-4267
888-999-RETA
http://www.reta.com/
RETA is an international society composed of men and women involved in the design, operation, and service of refrigeration and air-conditioning systems.

American Society for Testing and Materials (ASTM)
100 Barr Harbor Drive
West Conshohocken, PA 19428-2959
610-832-9585
http://www.astm.org/
The society promotes public health and safety, and the overall quality of life; contributes to the reliability of materials, products, systems and services.

NACE International
1440 South Creek Drive
Houston, TX 77084
281-228-6200
http://www.nace.org/
NACE International is a professional technical society dedicated to reducing the economic impact of corrosion.

Association for Computing Machinery (ACM)
One Asor Plaza
1515 Broadway
New York, NY 10036-5701
212-869-7440
http://www.acm.org/
ACM is an international scientific and educational organization dedicated to advancing the arts, sciences, and applications of information technology.

Society of Manufacturing Engineers (SME)
P.O. Box 930
Dearborn, MI 48121-0930
800-733-4763
http://www.sme.org/
The society is dedicated to serving its members and the manufacturing community through the advancement of professionalism, knowledge, and learning.

Societies within the SME
The Association for Electronics Manufacturing of the Society of Manufacturing Engineers (EM/SME)
P.O. Box 930
Dearborn, MI 48121-0930
800-733-4763
http://www.sme.org/
The society is dedicated to the advancement of the electronics manufacturing profession, keeping members up-to-date on the latest technical information and providing valuable opportunities for education and professional development.

Association for Forming and Fabricating Technologies of SME (AFFT/SME)
P.O. Box 930
Dearborn, MI 48121-0930
800-733-4SME
http://www.sme.org/
AFFT/SME adds value to members' professional development and serves the metal forming and fabricating community through educating, mentoring, networking, and providing a technology transfer forum.

Machine Vision Association of SME (MVA/SME)
P.O. Box 930
Dearborn, MI 48121-0930
800-733-4SME
http://www.sme.org/
MVA/SME serves its members' professional advancement by collecting and disseminating knowledge and experience about machine vision in the manufacturing process.

North American Manufacturing Research Institution of SME (NAMRI/SME)
P.O. Box 930
Dearborn, MI 48121-0930
800-733-4SME

http://www.sme.org/
NAMRI/SME serves individuals from industry and academia who are actively participating in research in manufacturing technology.

Plastics Molders and Manufacturers Association of SME (PMMA/SME)
P.O. Box 930
Dearborn, MI 48121-0930
800-733-4SME
http://www.sme.org/
PMMA/SME adds value to members' professional development and serves the plastics manufacturing community through educating, mentoring, networking, and providing a technology transfer forum.

Rapid Prototyping Association of SME (RPA/SME)
P.O. Box 930
Dearborn, MI 48121-0930
800-733-4SME
http://www.sme.org/
RPA/SME enhances members' and the manufacturing community's capabilities through interactive education of advanced rapid product development technologies.

Computer and Automated Systems Association of the Society of Manufacturing Engineers (CASA/SME)
P.O. Box 930
Dearborn, MI 48121-0930
800-733-4SME
http://www.sme.org/
CASA/SME is an information resource for professionals who are involved with automated and information systems in the manufacturing community.

Association for Finishing Processes of the Society of Manufacturing Engineers (AFP/SME)
P.O. Box 930
Dearborn, MI 48121-0930
800-733-4SME
http://www.sme.org/
AFP/SME provides an informational interchange among producers of coatings and pre-treatment applicators, product designers, equipment manufacturers, users, and coatings operations professionals, those responsible for environmental compliance, and finishing consultants.

Composites Manufacturing Association of the Society of Manufacturing Engineers (CMA/SME)
P.O. Box 930
Dearborn, MI 48121-0930
800-733-4SME
http://www.sme.org/
The society serves the composites manufacturing community by mentoring, networking, educating, and providing a technology transfer forum.

Machining Technology Association of the Society of Manufacturing Engineers (MTA/SME)
P.O. Box 930
Dearborn, MI 48121-0930
800-733-4SME
http://www.sme.org/
The society is dedicated to monitoring and assisting in the identification of technical developments, processes, and applications, and the potential impact on industry, and to help ensure that quality products and services are delivered by the Society that meet the needs and interests of the MTA/SME members.

Robotics International of the Society of Manufacturing Engineers (RI/SME)
P.O. Box 930
Dearborn, MI 48121-0930
800-733-4SME
http://www.sme.org/
The society is dedicated to the advancement of the robotics profession.

Society for Materials Engineering International (ASM)
9639 Kinsman RD
Materials Park, OH 44073-0002
800-336-5152
http://www.asm-intl.org/
The society is dedicated to advancing industry, technology, and applications of metals and materials.

National Association of Power Engineers (NAPE)
1 Springfield Street
Chicopee, MA 01013
413-592-NAPE
http://www.powerengineers.com/
The society is dedicated to the principles of education, knowledge, training, and career enhancement for its members.

Society of Tribologists and Lubrication Engineers (STLE)
840 Busse Hwy
Park Ridge, IL 60068-2376
847-825-5536
http://www.stle.org/
The society advances the science and technology of lubrication (tribology).

Fluid Power Society (FPS)
2433 N. Mayfair Road, Ste. 111
Milwaukee, WI 53226
414-257-0910
http://www.ifps.org/
Society services include education, certification, and professionalism for fluid power and motion control professionals.

American Welding Society (AWS)
550 LeJeune Rd. NW
Miami, FL 33126
800-443-9353
http://www.aws.org/
AWS provides quality products and services to members and the industry which will advance the science, technology, and applications of materials joining throughout the world.

Industrial Engineering
Institute of Industrial Engineers (IIE)
25 Technology Park/ Atlanta
Norcross, GA 30092
800-494-0460
http://www.iienet.org/IIE1.htm
IIE provides leadership in developing industrial engineering; enhancing the capabilities of those who are involved in or manage the application, education, training, research, or development of industrial engineering; and, representing the industrial engineering profession.

Societies within the IIE
Society for Health Systems
http://www.iienet.org/sdig/sdig1g.htm#Society for Health Systems
The society exists to enhance career development and education as a professional working in the health care systems and services industry.

Society for Engineering and Management Systems (SEMS)
http://www.iienet.org/sdig/sdig1g.htm#Engineering and Management
The society was created to help managers at every level to improve productivity and quality, through effective and economical managerial techniques and philosophies.

Society for Work Science (Ergonomics and Work Measurement) (SWS)
http://www.iienet.org/sdig/sdig1g.htm#Ergonomics and Work Measurement
The division appeals to IEs involved in increasing productivity, quality, and safety through job redesign.

Divisions within the IIE
All divisions can be found at the website
http://www.iienet.org/sdig/sdig1g.htm or by contacting the IIE directly.

Aerospace and Defense Division supports employees in aerospace and defense industries who are involved in "just-in-time" manufacturing, total quality improvement, computer-integrated manufacturing, implementing statistical methods, simulation, and work measurement.

Energy, Environment and Plant Engineering Division supports industrial engineers who are responsible for energy management, environmental protection, and plant engineering.

Engineering Economy Division members are involved in economic and investment analysis.

Facilities Planning and Design Division provides a forum for IEs involved in planning and designing manufacturing and service-related facilities including plants, warehouses, office buildings, and hospitals.

Financial Services Division includes professionals intent on the improvement of the operational performance of banks, savings institutions, and other financial organizations.

Logistics Transportation and Distribution Division unites industrial engineers involved in various modes of transportation services, including railroads, transit systems, trucking, and air transport.

Manufacturing Division represents IE's who continually endeavor to increase productivity, streamline manufacturing processes, and integrate those systems necessary for producing products in a cost-efficient manner.

Operations Research Division members apply mathematics and sophisticated computer programs to solve engineering problems.

Quality Control and Engineering Reliability Division supports professionals undertaking total quality management, quality measurement and assurance, quality control analysis, inspection criteria, and reliability/maintainability of products or services.

Utilities Division includes industrial engineers who work inthe public utilities industry; for example, the water, gas or nuclear trades.

Human Factors and Ergonomics Society (HFES)
P.O. Box 1369
Santa Monica, CA 90406-1369
310-394-1811
http://www.hfes.org/
The society promotes the discovery and exchange of knowledge concerning the characteristics of human beings that are applicable to the design of systems and devices of all kinds.

Society of Logistics Engineers (SOLE)
8100 Professional Pl., Ste. 211
Hyattsville, MD 20785
301-459-8446
http://www.sole.org/
The society engages in scientific, educational, and literary endeavors to enhance the art of logistics technology, education, and management.

Nuclear Engineering Societies
American Nuclear Society (ANS)
555 N. Kensington Ave
La Grange Park, IL 60526
708-352-6611
http://www.ans.org/
ANS was established by a group of individuals who recognized the need to unify the professional activities within the diverse fields of nuclear science and technology.

Technical Divisions within the ANS can be found at the website http://www.ans.org/prof.divs/
Accelerator Applications Technical Group
The Technical Group was organized to promote the advancement of knowledge of the use of particle accelerator technologies for nuclear and other applications.

Biology and Medicine Division
Members focus on the application and development of nuclear technology for the life sciences, as well as the impact of such technology on society.

Decommissioning, Decontamination, and Reutilization (DD&R)
DD&R provides an overall focus for presentation and technological advancement of the programmatic aspects of this technology.

Education and Training Division
Through the exchange of views andinformation on matters related to
education and training in nuclear science, engineering, and technology, this division links the academic, industrial, and governmental communities.

Environmental Sciences Division
Information on the relationship of nuclear power to the environment,
the ecological influence of nuclear processes, and the trade-offs of nuclear
technology in relation to other sciences are studied and disseminated
by division members.

Fuel Cycle and Waste Management Division
Devoted to all aspects of the nuclear fuel cycle including waste management worldwide.

Fusion Energy
This division promotes the development and timely introduction of fusion energy as a sustainable energy source with favorable economic,
environmental, and safety attributes.

Human Factors Division
Improving task performance, system reliability, system and personel
safety, efficiency, and effectiveness are the division's main objectives.

Isotopes and Radiation Division
Members are devoted to applying nuclear science and engineering technologies involving isotopes, radiation applications, and assorted equipment in scientific research, development, and industrial processes.

Materials Science and Technology Division (MSTD)
The objectives of MSTD are to promote the advancement of materials
science in nuclear science technology; support the multidisciplines which
constitute it; encourage research by providing a forum for the presentation, exchange, and documentation of relevant information.

Mathematics and Computation Division
Division members promote the advancement of mathematical and computational methods for solving problems arising in all disciplines en-
compassed by the Society.

Nuclear Criticality Safety Division (NCSD)
NCSD provides communication among nuclear criticality safety professionals through the development of standards, the evolution of training methods and materials, the presentation of technical data and procedures, and the creation of specialty publications.

Nuclear Operations
Division members distribute information pertinent to the operation, use, and management of nuclear reactors and of associated equipment, the facilities, and techniques required for and peculiar to the operation and maintenance of critical facilities, research and test reactors, power reactors, process heat reactors, propulsion reactors, and reactors for other purposes as may be developed.

Nuclear Installations Safety Division
The division is devoted specifically to the safety of nuclear reactors and the health and safety of the public, this division seeks a better understanding of the role of safety in the design, construction, and operation of nuclear reactor facilities.

Power Division
Members concentrate on applied nuclear science and engineering related to nuclear power plants (e.g. design, operation, maintenance, economics, management, and licensing).

Radiation Protection and Shielding Division
The division promotes the interchange of technology related to the transport of particulate and electromagnetic radiation in materials and biological systems; techniques and instrumentation to measure and calculate radiation fields; and the quantification of radiation effects and nuclear heat deposition within materials.

Reactor Physics Division
The division's objectives are to promote the advancement of knowledge and understanding of the fundamental physical phenomena characterizing nuclear reactors and other nuclear systems.

Robotics and Remote Systems Division
Members are interested in the advancement of science and engineering related to remotely operated systems, facilities, equipment, and devices for nuclear energy and other related applications.

Thermal Hydraulics Division
The division provides a forum for focused technical dialogue on thermal hydraulic technology in the nuclear industry.

Society of Nuclear Medicine
1850 Samuel Morse Drive
Reston, VA 20190
(703) 708-9000
http://www.snm.org/
The society advances excellence in health care through support of education and research in nuclear medicine.

Index

Symbols

3M 42

A

AAAI 157
AAAS 163
AAEE 14, 74
AAES 158
AAF 148
AAMI 141
AAS 164
ABET 18, 27
Academic preparation 19
Academics 27
Accelerated Programs 28
Accreditation Board for Engineering and Technology *see ABET*
ACEC 159
ACerS 144
ACM 171
ACS 142
ACT 19
Adams, Scott   14, 54
adaptable 10
admissions 18
Adobe 80
AEE 145
AEF 164
AEG 149
Aeronautical Engineering 39, 88
Aerospace Engineering 88
AES 157
AESS 151
Africa 74
Agricultural Engineering 85

AHA 145
AIA 149
AIAA 164
AIChE 14, 64
air flow 73
Air Force 27
air transportation 20
airplanes 15
AISC 148
AISE 149
AISES 159
Alabama 105
Alaska 106
algebra 19
Allaire, Paul   42
Allen, Wayne 42
all-star job 11
American Association for Engineering Education *see AAEE*
American dream 10
American Institute of Chemical Engineers *see AIChE*
American Medical Association 16
American Nuclear Society *see ANS*
American Society of Mechanical Engineers *see ASME*
Anderson, Mary 33
Anne Perusek 32
ANS 3, 101
antisocial-nerd 11
aptitude 19
Architectural Engineering 72, 145
Arizona 106
Arkansas 107

U

U.S. Department of Education 10
U.S. Secretary of Education 10
understanding nature 15
underwater societies 96
underwater structures 84
Utah 137

V

versatile 10
Virginia 52, 138, 139
volcano 96
VTS 156

W

Wall Street 17
Walt Disney 47
Wang, Jaw-Kai 86
want-ads 10
Washington
35, 51, 52, 139, 141, 142, 144,
148, 149, 158, 159, 163, 165, 166
Washington, George 41, 50
water and waste systems 63
water distribution system 73
Watt, James 51
Welch, Jack 42
West Virginia 139
what is engineering? 14
wheelchairs 59
Wichita State University 21
Widnall, Sheila E. 35
Williams, Montel 54
Wisconsin 104, 139, 140, 161
women 11, 30, 105
workforce 14
Wright Brothers 40, 42, 88
writer 17
Wyoming 41, 74

X

Xerox 42

Order Form

Postal Orders:
Bonamy Publishing
P.O. Box 673, Calhoun, LA 71225
Tel: (318) 644-0532
Fax: (318) 644-0532

Please send the following books:
I understand that I may return any books for a full refund - for
any reason, no questions asked.

_____ copy/copies of **Is There an Engineer Inside
You?** at 14.95 each.

Sales Tax:
Please add 8.5% for books shipped to
Louisiana addresses.

Shipping:
$4.00 for the first book and $2.00 for each
additional book

Payment:
Please send Checks or Money Orders only.

Amount enclosed_____

Order Form

Postal Orders:
Bonamy Publishing
P.O. Box 673, Calhoun, LA 71225
Tel: (318) 644-0532
Fax: (318) 644-0532

Please send the following books:
I understand that I may return any books for a full refund - for
any reason, no questions asked.

_____ copy/copies of **Is There an Engineer Inside
You?** at 14.95 each.

Sales Tax:
Please add 8.5% for books shipped to
Louisiana addresses.

Shipping:
$4.00 for the first book and $2.00 for each
additional book

Payment:
Please send Checks or Money Orders only.

Amount enclosed_____